The Madness of Queen Maria

Jenifer Roberts is the author of *Glass: The Strange History of the Lyne Stephens Fortune*, published by Templeton Press in 2003.

A book of her landscape photography, *Spirit of the Place*, was published by Creative Monochrome in 1992.

She lives in an old farmhouse in Wiltshire with her husband and a rescue dog.

The Madness of Queen Maria

The Remarkable Life of
Maria I of Portugal

JENIFER ROBERTS

TEMPLETON PRESS

First published in 2009
by Templeton Press

A CIP catalogue record for this book
is available from the British Library.

ISBN 978–0–9545589–1–8

Designed by Linda Reed & Associates, Shaftesbury
Printed and bound in Great Britain by
CPI Antony Rowe, Chippenham and Eastbourne

Templeton Press
42 The Common, Langley Burrell,
Chippenham SN15 4LQ

For Paul

Contents

Illustrations ix

Introduction xi

Family Trees: Bragança and Bourbon families xvi

Maps: Central Portugal and Lisbon area xviii

PROLOGUE 1

PART ONE: CROWN PRINCESS

1 A Royal Childhood 5

2 Princess of Brazil 12

3 Earthquake 19

4 The Rise of Pombal 25

5 A Quiet Wedding 31

6 Nuptial Felicity 38

7 The Succession 46

PART TWO: ABSOLUTE POWER

8 Regime Change 57

9 The Shadow of Pombal 64

10 The Double Marriage 70

11 Bereavement 77

12 Crisis in Cabinet 84

13 English Hospitality 89

PART THREE: A FRAGILE MIND

14 A String of Tragedies 101

15 On the Brink 107

16 A Private Hell 113

17 The Gathering Storm 122

18 Exile 129

19 Return to Portugal 136

EPILOGUE 141

APPENDICES

Account of the royal visit to Marinha Grande, Philadelphia Stephens, 25 July 1788 145

Glossary 159

Cast of characters 162

Reference notes 170

Select bibliography 172

Index 176

Illustrations

Front cover

Maria as crown princess, c.1753. Painting attributed to Francisco Vieira de Matos (Vieira Lusitano). *Palácio Nacional de Queluz/photograph by Manuel Palma/Divisão de Documentação Fotográfica, Instituto dos Museus et da Conservação, I P.*

Back cover

Bookplate of Maria I. Steel engraving by Jerónimo de Barros Ferreira.

Plate Section

1 Terreiro do Paço and the royal palace in Lisbon, 1693. *Coleção de Jorge de Brito, Cascais.*

2 Garden façade of the palace of Queluz, built by Pedro 1747–1752.

3 Marquis de Pombal, c.1769. Painting attributed to Joana da Salitre. *Museu da Cidade – Câmara Municipal da Lisboa.*

4 Maria I and Pedro III, 1777. Unknown artist. *Museu Nacional dos Coches/photograph by José Pessoa/Divisão de Documentação Fotográfica, Instituto dos Museus et da Conservação, I P.*

5 Maria I. Engraving by Marie Anne Bourlier from original miniature portrait, probably by Daniel Valentine Rivière, published in London in October 1807. © *National Portrait Gallery, London.*

6 Prince José, c.1777. Unknown artist. *Museu Nacional dos Coches/Divisão de Documentação Fotográfica, Instituto dos Museus et da Conservação, I P.*

7 Benedita, sister of Maria I and wife of Crown Prince José, c.1785. Painting attributed to Jean Baptiste Debret. *Museu Nacional dos Coches/Divisão de Documentação Fotográfica, Instituto dos Museus et da Conservação, I P.*

8 Carlota Joaquina, c.1785. Copy of original portrait by Mariano Salvador Maella in the Prado Museum, Madrid. *Palácio Nacional de Queluz/photograph by Paulo Cintra/Laura Castro Caldas/ Divisão de Documentação Fotográfica, Instituto dos Museus et da Conservação, I P.*

9 Prince João, c.1799. Engraving from original portrait by D Pelegrim, published in London in 1815. *Private collection.*

10 Maria I. Painting (in original frame) by Guiseppe Troni, probably a copy of the portrait painted from life by Thomas Hickey in 1783. *Palácio Nacional de Queluz/photograph by José Pessoa/Divisão de Documentação Fotográfica, Instituto dos Museus et da Conservação, I P.*

11 Dr Francis Willis, 1789. Painting by John Russell. *© National Portrait Gallery, London.*

12 William Stephens of Marinha Grande. Engraving by A Smith after drawing by Bouck, published in London in 1799. *Private collection.*

13 Stephens's mansion house in Marinha Grande. *Câmara Municipal da Marinha Grande.*

14 Dona Maria Pavilion at the palace of Queluz. *Photograph by Luís Pavão.*

15 Largo do Paço, Rio de Janeiro, early 19th century. Painting by J Steinmann, published in Edmundo, Luís, *A Côrte de D. João no Rio de Janeiro*, 1939. *© British Library Board. All Rights Reserved (X700/456).*

Introduction

She is truly worthy of esteem and respect but she has not the qualities that make a great queen. No-one can be kinder, more charitable or more sensitive, but these good qualities are marred by an excessive religious devotion.
Duke du Châtelet, 1777

Maria I of Portugal has been treated unkindly by history. Some writers dismiss her as nothing more than a religious nutcase. Others relegate her years on the throne to a footnote, sandwiched between the more dramatic periods of the Marquis de Pombal and the Peninsular War. She deserves better than this, not only because she was a good woman whose misfortune was to inherit the crown, but also because her story is a graphic example of the 18th-century battle between church and state, between the old superstitions and the age of reason.

Maria embodied these contradictions. Pulled by her instincts towards the old religion, she understood at least some aspects of the Enlightenment and took a humanitarian approach to state affairs. A weak and fragile woman, she was unsuited for monarchy and the struggle for power between church and state helped to destroy her.

Although she did her best to rule the country with the advice of her ministers, Maria had little interest in politics. I have therefore not written a political history, concentrating instead on the difficulties in her private life, as well as on the major events and personalities of her era.

The most useful contemporary source was the correspondence of the British envoys in Lisbon, particularly the Hon. Robert Walpole (nephew of Sir Robert Walpole, first minister of England) who wrote such informative and entertaining letters. I enjoyed his company as I worked my way through the state and Foreign Office papers in the National Archives and missed him when he went home on leave. Another fruitful source was the journal of the Marquis de Bombelles, French ambassador to Portugal during the years 1786–1788, who was so deliciously indiscreet in the private pages of his diary.

In the summer of 1788, Maria spent three days at the royal glassworks in Marinha Grande, a factory owned by an Englishman, William Stephens. A few weeks later, his sister (Philadelphia) wrote a letter describing this unique event in royal history, a letter which has only recently come to light. Her correspondent was Thomas Cogan, a cousin in London, who kept the letter amongst his private papers. When he died in 1792, it passed to his son, Thomas White Cogan, who became rector of East Dean in Sussex and died in 1856. More than a century later, it was presented to the West Sussex Record Office as part of 'the residue of Mr W P Cogan's records as a solicitor', having been found in a house in Chichester in the early 1960s.

While Philadelphia's letter lay undisturbed in the archives, I wrote a book about William Stephens and the wealth he accumulated at Marinha Grande (*Glass: The Strange History of the Lyne Stephens Fortune*). I quoted from the memoirs of Dr William Withering who visited the factory in 1793:

> Mr Stephens had the honour to entertain the queen and royal family of Portugal for three days in 1788. Her Majesty's attendants, together with the vast influx of persons from the surrounding countryside, formed an assembly of many thousands. Thirty-two cooks were employed and stabling provided for eight hundred and fifty-three horses and mules. To the credit of Portuguese honesty and sobriety, only two silver spoons were lost from sixty dozens in use and, although wine was placed in the apartments used by the servants, not a man was seen intoxicated.[1]

Apart from a brief mention of 'the queen's visit' in the accounts book at Marinha Grande, this was the only reference I could find to an occasion which seemed so extraordinary. Dr Withering – a member of the Lunar Society of Birmingham – has the reputation of a careful and thorough man. No-one could accuse him of exaggeration but I did wonder whether his memory had served him correctly.

The Stephens family came from Devon and Cornwall. Geography had not led me to the West Sussex Record Office but, after the publication of *Glass*, the curator added some additional manuscripts to the Access to Archives website (an on-going project which collates the catalogues of record offices throughout the country). And one day, idly typing 'Marinha Grande' into the website, I found the following reference: 'Account by Philadelphia Stephens of a Visit by the Queen and Royal Family of Portugal to Marinha Grande, 25 July 1788.'

Glass was inspired by my admiration for William Stephens. *The Madness of Queen Maria* was inspired by his sister, whose account of the royal visit provides an intimate glimpse into the world of absolute monarchy – a snapshot of court life in the old Europe – just one year before the French Revolution began to change the face of the continent. It also gives a sympathetic portrait of Maria during her last few weeks of happiness, before she suffered the string of tragedies that would lead to the onset of insanity – and to the unfortunate name of *Maria A Louca*, Maria the Mad.

Names and Titles

Portuguese spelling has been used for members of the Bragança family. Names of Spanish kings have been anglicised as they are better known to English readers as Philip, Ferdinand and Charles.

A major figure in the story is Sebastião José de Carvalho e Melo, known to history as the Marquis de Pombal. He used the name Carvalho until he was given the title of Count de Oeiras in 1759. Ten years later, he was created 1st Marquis de Pombal. With a few exceptions at the beginning of the story, the name Pombal has been used throughout. The same applies to Maria's first minister, the Viscount de Ponte de Lima (whose previous title was Viscount de Vila Nova da Cerveira).

It was the custom in some noble families to have two concurrent titles. During the lifetime of the 3rd Marquis de Távora, his eldest son used the title of 4th Marquis de Távora. They were known respectively as 'the old marquis' and 'the young marquis'. Their wives were similarly known as 'the old marquesa' and 'the young marquesa'.

It was common practice for a man to attach his mother's maiden name to his paternal surname, linking the two with 'e' (Carvalho e Melo, Seabra e Silva, Melo e Castro). Such men were normally referred to by the first of these names (Carvalho, Seabra, Melo).

Currency & Exchange Rates

The basic unit of Portuguese currency was the *real*, a unit of insignificant value. One thousand *reis* (plural of *real*) formed a *milreis*. The *cruzado* was worth 400 *reis*, the *moydore* ten times this amount: 4000 *reis* or 4 *milreis*.

During the period of this story, the English pound was worth just over three and a half *milreis*. Varying values of the pound sterling are not a reliable indicator of present-day values of Portuguese currency, but to give an idea of scale, £1 in 1750 would be worth £160 today. This figure declined to £131 in 1770, to £108 in 1790, and to £66 in 1807.

Appendices

The account by Philadelphia Stephens of the royal visit to Marinha Grande is transcribed in full on pages 145–158. A glossary of Portuguese and archaic English words quoted in the text follows on pages 159–161.

Members of the royal family often used the same name (João, José, Mariana), while Portuguese names can be confusing to the English reader. For easy reference, a list of the major figures in the story is given on pages 162–169.

Quotations

To reduce the number of references in the text, quotations from British envoys and consuls are not referenced individually. Their letters can be found (in date order) in the National Archives at Kew, series SP 89 for years up to and including 1780; series FO 63 thereafter.

Acknowledgements

I should like to thank Dr José Pedro Barosa, who inspired my interest in Marinha Grande and helped with the more archaic references in the account of Maria's visit to the glassworks. Thanks are also due to Luís de Abreu e Sousa, for research into the accounts book at Marinha Grande; to Christine Robinson, for translations of letters and documents; and to W Stephen Gilbert, Hilary Green, and Peter and Yvonne Taylor, for reading the manuscript and for their many helpful suggestions.

Permission to reproduce original material has been granted by the West Sussex Record Office. I should also like to thank Oxford University Press for permission to use 43 words from *Journals of a Residence in Portugal 1800–1801 and a Visit to France 1838* by Robert Southey (edited by Adolfo Cabral, Clarendon Press, 1960).

I am – as always – deeply grateful to my husband for his patience over the years, his company and his help on most of my travels, and his tolerance as I worked long hours on the manuscript. I owe him far more than these words can express.

THE ROYAL HOUSE OF BRAGANÇA

(Portuguese monarchs in bold)

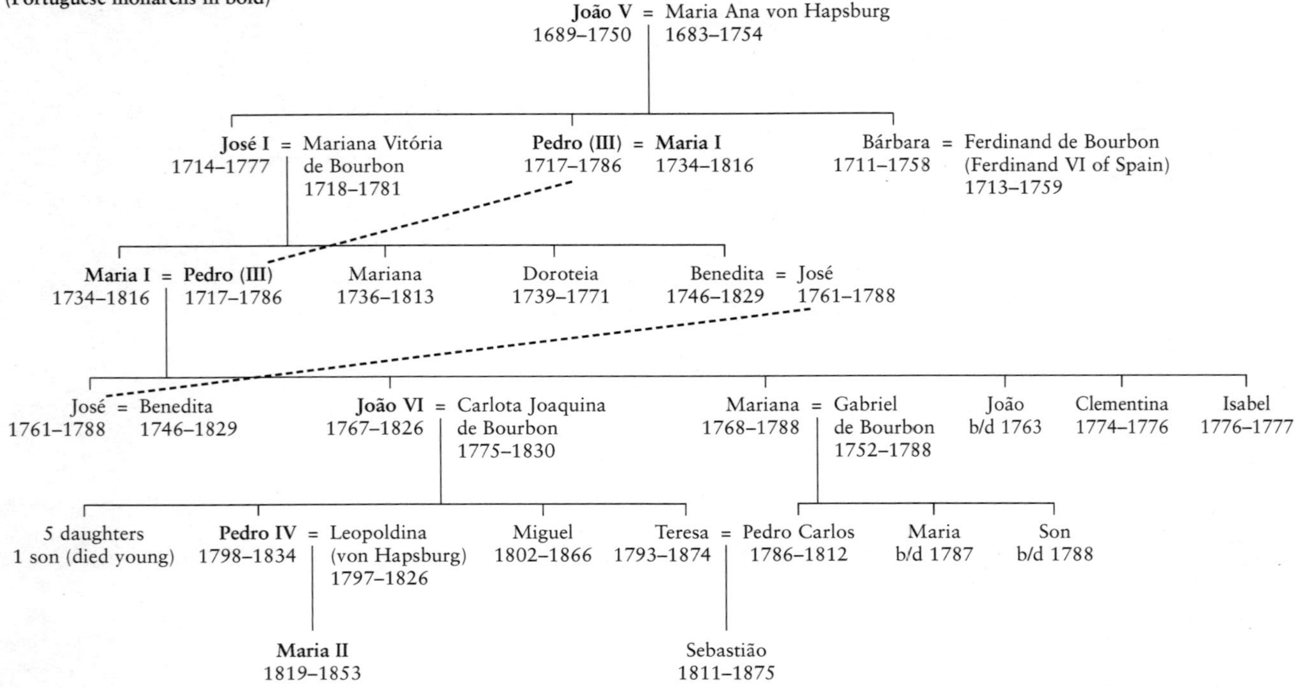

THE ROYAL HOUSE OF BOURBON
(Spanish monarchs in bold)

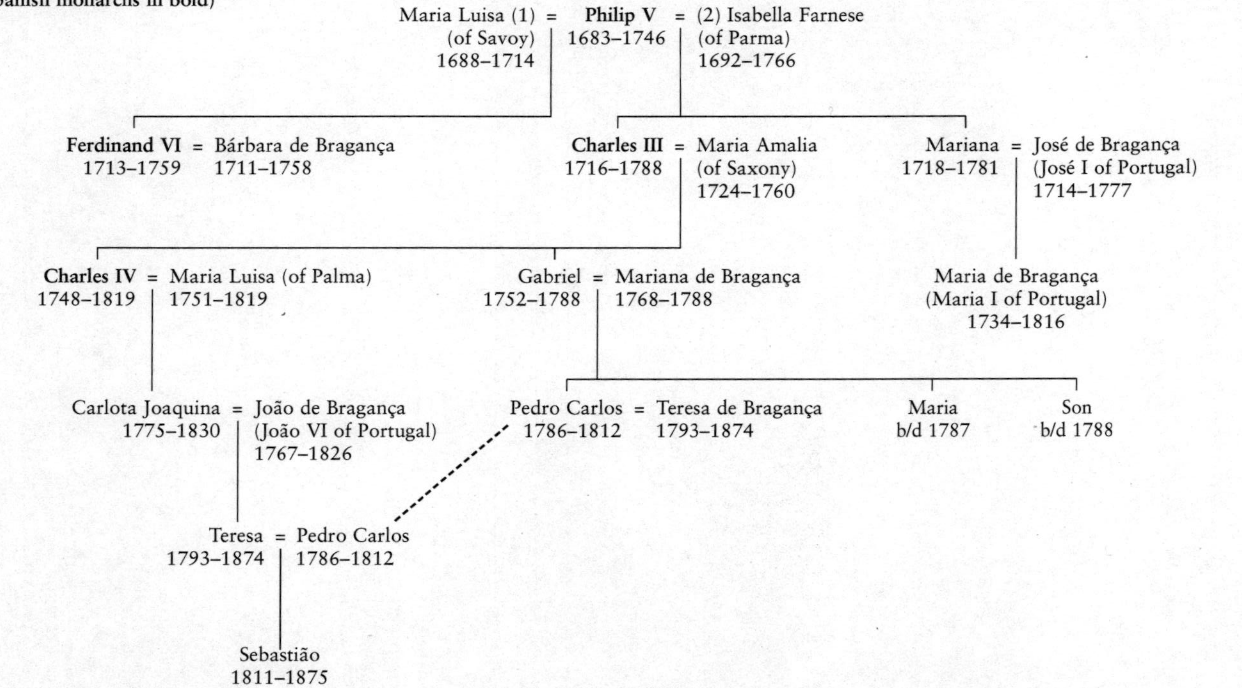

Central Portugal

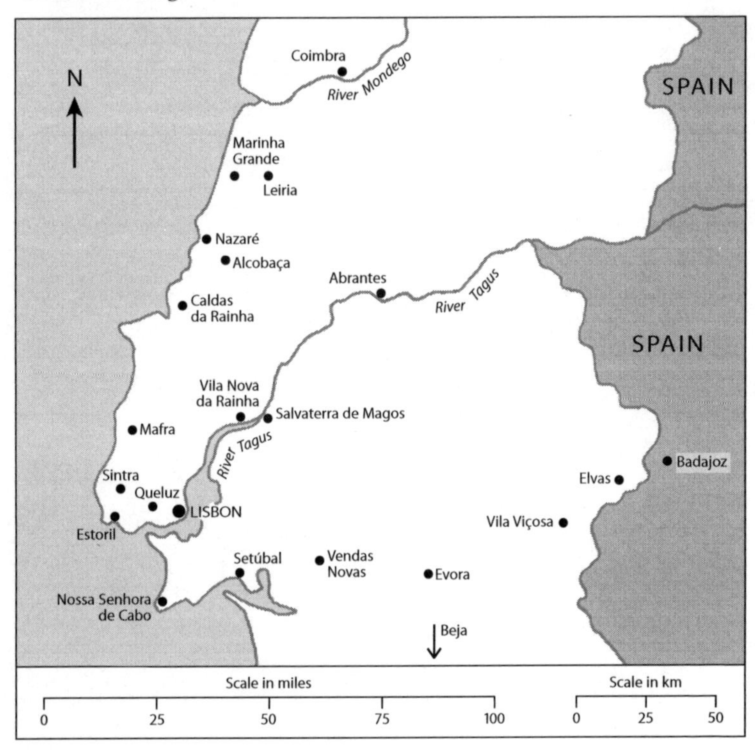

Lisbon area

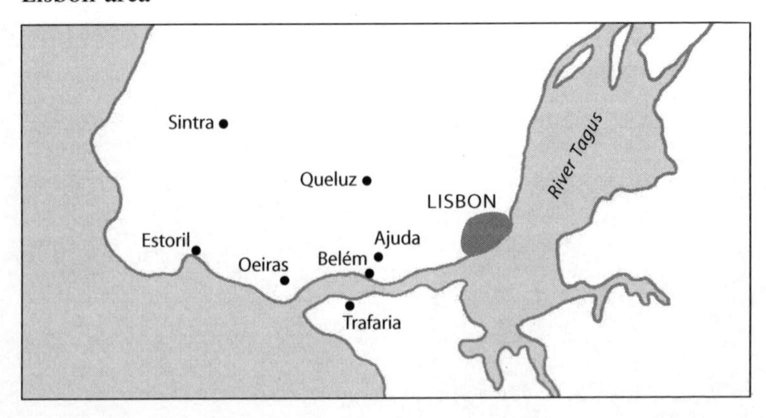

Indeed, history is nothing more than
a tableau of crimes and misfortunes.

Voltaire
(*L'Ingénu*, 1767)

Prologue

3 February 1792

The royal palace at Salvaterra was in a state of panic when the sky first lightened on a winter morning in 1792. Nobody had slept that night. Fires still burnt in the braziers, candelabras threw shadows on the walls, and a group of doctors spoke in low voices to an agitated young man of twenty-four. João de Bragança, crown prince of Portugal, felt utterly helpless. An indecisive young man at the best of times, he had no idea what to do in such an unprecedented situation.

The previous evening, during a performance in the palace theatre, his mother – the reigning queen – had finally lost her senses. She had shrieked and howled through the night and now she was pacing the floor, tearing at her hair and her clothes, screaming in fear and distress. Her attendants clustered around her. They did their best to calm her but they were terrified of touching the royal person, of flouting royal protocol.

The morning dawned overcast and grey. Rain had been falling for several days, the damp permeating the rooms of the palace. Servants bustled about the apartments, packing the royal wardrobes, preparing to take the queen home to Lisbon. On the river, the royal barge – the *Bergantim Real* – was cleaned and polished, the gold dragon on the prow shining bright through the morning drizzle. Footmen prepared the gilded cabin with rugs and red velvet cushions. Eighty oarsmen dressed themselves in resplendent livery of red and yellow. A light meal – a *merenda* – was prepared in the kitchens and carried on board, plates of exquisitely-prepared food, flagons of spring water, wine and lemonade.

When everything was ready, the queen was brought from the palace, flanked by her two sisters who held tightly onto her arms, followed by her son with an expression of despair on his face. With a canopy held above her head to protect her from the rain, she was led to the river bank and settled onto the velvet cushions in the cabin. The rowers dipped their oars in the water, the barge moved slowly out into the river Tagus.

The journey to Lisbon took several hours. And when the *Bergantim Real* arrived in the city, the great square by the waterside was crowded with people who had heard rumours of the queen's 'indisposition' and come to see their sovereign. Forty oars were raised to the vertical, the barge came to a halt at the quayside, and the distraught woman was bustled into a waiting carriage and taken across the square to the Senate House. A short time later, her pale face appeared at a window overlooking the square, greeted by cheers from the crowds below.

The following evening, the severity of her condition was announced to the public. Bells tolled, sacred images were brought to her apartments, religious processions moved through the streets. Prayers 'for the precious health of Her Majesty' were intoned night and day in every church and convent in the city. But as the queen herself put it, neither doctors nor priests could reverse the decrees of fate.

Part One

Crown Princess

1

A Royal Childhood

He who never saw Lisbon never saw a fine thing.
Old Portuguese proverb

Fifty-seven years earlier, the great square on the Lisbon waterside – the Terreiro do Paço – was the scene of much rejoicing. It was another damp winter afternoon. Squalls blew in from the river and the rain lay in puddles in the square and on the marble-faced quay by the waterside. To the west, the palace of the Bragança family stood grandiose and proud. The rooms and corridors were lit with candelabras and thick tallow torches, and servants hurried about with containers of hot water and clean linen. A sixteen-year-old princess was giving birth to her first child.

At six o'clock in the evening, as she pushed and groaned for the last time, a daughter was born, a child who would grow up to become the first female monarch in Portuguese history. According to custom, the infant emerged from her mother's body in full view of a bevy of priests, courtiers, ministers, doctors and attendants. She was gathered into the arms of her grandmother, taken into an adjacent room, and presented to her grandfather (King João V) and her father (Crown Prince José), who fell to their knees to give thanks to God for a safe delivery.

Large numbers of people were gathered in the Terreiro do Paço. When the news was announced, the air reverberated with cheering crowds, pealing bells and cannon-fire. Soon the carriages of foreign diplomats arrived at the palace. 'I immediately went to court,' the British envoy wrote to London that night, 'for I was told it was the custom to do so, and had audiences with the royal family to congratulate them on the occasion. I recommend that the king's letter of congratulation may not be deferred a moment but sent by the next packet boat as this court is very punctilious in these sorts of affairs.'

The celebrations continued for three days. Firecrackers rose into the sky, bells continued to peal, and as darkness fell, the people of Lisbon placed lighted candles in their windows, illuminating the city at night. The *Te Deum* was sung in the churches and, on 9 January 1735, the infant was carried to chapel and baptised – 'with great pomp and ceremony' – Maria Francisca Isabel Josefa Antónia Gertrudes Rita Joana de Bragança.

Maria was born in the richest and most opulent city in Europe, a Lisbon enriched by the gold and diamond mines of Brazil. Every year, treasure fleets arrived from Rio de Janeiro with cargoes of precious stones and metals, wealth used by her grandfather to enrich the Portuguese church until it rivalled the Vatican in pomp and splendour.

In theory, João V was a monarch with absolute power. In practice, he was totally in thrall to the priesthood. The church was the most powerful institution in the country, indulged by the king until no-one knew where ecclesiastical authority ended and royal authority began. The Society of Jesus held a pre-eminent position. Jesuits controlled the entire system of education, acted as confessors to all members of the royal family, and zealous in the defence of the Catholic faith, had built up a considerable power base in the country.

The Archbishop of Lisbon (known as the Patriarch) had been elevated to the rank of pontiff. He wore similar vestments to the Pope and was attended by a Sacred College of twenty-four prelates dressed in scarlet robes. 'There is no ecclesiastic in the world,' wrote Joseph Baretti, friend of Dr Johnson, 'who is surrounded with so great a pomp as this Patriarch.'[1]

The king built convents and churches, lined them with rare marble and stuffed them with treasure: gold and silver altars studded with precious stones, paintings and sculpture from Italy, libraries with tens of thousands of books. 'His gaieties were religious processions,' wrote Voltaire. 'When he took to building, he built monasteries; when he wanted a mistress, he chose a nun.'[2] João's favourite convent was the nunnery of Odivelas, where he kept an apartment lined with carpets and mirrors. Two of his many bastard children were conceived here.

Meanwhile his wife, Maria Ana of Austria, bore him six legitimate children, three of whom survived to adulthood: Bárbara, José and Pedro. In a double ceremony on the Spanish border in 1729, Bárbara married Ferdinand de Bourbon (crown prince of Spain), and Crown Prince José married Ferdinand's ten-year-old sister, Mariana. This was one of the most glittering occasions in Portuguese history. 'Everybody knows,' wrote a British envoy thirty years later, 'that the immense cost of clothes and equipage when the double marriage was celebrated at the frontier of Spain depressed the noble families for many years; some have not yet recovered from that wound.'

José's wife reached puberty in 1732. He joined her in the marriage bed and soon the court was waiting anxiously for news. The Bragança succession depended on Mariana's fertility and there was great rejoicing when – after a wait of two years – it was announced that she was at last expecting a child. Maria was born on 17 December 1734 and, during the next twelve years, the royal couple produced three more daughters: Mariana, Doroteia and Benedita.

The four sisters grew up together at court, spending much of their time in Lisbon. The south façade of the palace overlooked a harbour three miles wide, a harbour always full of shipping. To the east lay the Terreiro do Paço, the meeting place of the city. Religious processions passed through the square, the people of Lisbon strolled on the marble-faced quay by the waterfront, and bullfights were held here on Sunday afternoons.

Processions of hooded penitents gathered in the square during Holy Week, 'bare-footed, with long heavy chains attached to their ankles which made a dismal rattling'. They carried stones or crosses on their backs and whipped themselves 'so hard their backs were red and swollen from the violence and repetition of the blows'.[3] And twice a year, in *autos-da-fé* attended 'with great diligence' by Maria's grandfather and members of the court, the square was filled with torches and flaming pyres as victims of the Holy Inquisition were garrotted and burned beneath the palace windows.

Religious imagery, the violent and the beautiful, filled the days of Maria's childhood. She spent long hours at her devotions, enthralled by the ritual, transported with pleasure as the royal musicians played and sang in richly-ornamented churches. She attended morning mass and evening prayers in the palace chapel and there was a saint's day or religious festival at least once a week. Maria sat by her mother's side in church and, at every service, Mariana would kiss the pages of her prayer book, 'it being her custom to kiss the names of God, our blessed Lady, and all the saints and angels in any book that she opens'.[4]

They attended religious festivals in the countryside too, where João had several palaces with hunting parks which allowed his family to indulge their passion for blood sports. The immense convent-palace in Mafra, which housed royal apartments as well as several hundred Franciscan friars, was built by João to fulfil a vow made on his wedding night, that he would build a convent dedicated to St Francis if his wife gave him children. The palace in Belém (three miles west of Lisbon) had an indoor riding school where the royal horses were trained and Maria learned her skills on horseback. The Moorish palace in the hills of Sintra offered escape from the summer heat, and the hunting parks at Salvaterra de Magos and Vila Viçosa provided excellent sport.

When the family travelled from one palace to another, their furniture and furnishings travelled with them: beds, tables and chairs, tapestries and rugs, mirrors, dinner services, silver and glassware. 'The court cannot move a step without taking its furniture along with it,' wrote a Frenchman who lived in Lisbon, 'for the family has none in more than one place at a time and cannot change abode without carrying it all along with them, even down to their beds and bedding.'[5]

Large numbers of carriages, chaises and carts ('a prodigious number of vehicles, a medley of carriages old and new') were requisitioned for each journey, as well as horses and mules for the stages on the road. And when they arrived at their destination, the servants worked at speed to prepare the accommodation. Beds were assembled, furniture arranged, wall coverings hung, rugs laid on the floor. Cooks sweated in the kitchens to prepare the first meal, attendants unpacked the royal wardrobes. In the stables, the horses and tack were prepared and polished for the family would be up early next morning, keen to mount their horses and follow the chase.

When Maria was seven years old, her grandfather suffered a massive stroke which paralysed the entire left side of his body. Prayers were read in the churches and convents, state affairs came to a standstill, and 'religious processions filled the streets night and day from the instant he was taken ill'. The doctors advised him to take the baths at Caldas da Rainha in the hope that immersion in hot sulphurous waters would help to restore his health. It was a ten-hour journey to the spa town and the family set out on 9 July 1742, travelling on barges up the Tagus to Vila Nova da Rainha where carriages were waiting to take them overland to Caldas.

They returned to Lisbon on 17 August. Six weeks later, the king had another attack, 'a fainting fit which deprived him of his senses for half an hour'. All public appearances were cancelled but he insisted on attending an *auto-da-fé* on 4 November, an event which lasted for fourteen hours and 'was a source of fatigue to several in better health who were obliged to attend'. João had a third stroke on 12 November and, for the rest of his life, he suffered from 'violent seizures' every few weeks, sometimes for days at a time.

This put an end to visits to country palaces, although the doctors still believed in the beneficial effect of the baths and his family accompanied him to Caldas thirteen times in eight years. Each time they made the journey, the royal furniture and furnishings travelled with them and, when the king had a stroke on the road, the entire entourage had to turn around and head back to Lisbon.

The queen acted as regent whenever João was too ill to meet with his ministers, but mostly he kept matters of state to himself. There were complaints about Maria Ana's inexperience, while the nobility hoped that Crown Prince José would take a more active role in government. The king refused to allow it. 'His Majesty has become so very infirm,' wrote the British consul, 'as at best to only doze, being mighty peevish, dispatching nothing, and yet will have everything go through his hands.'[6]

As his health deteriorated, João spent his days attending divine service in the patriarchal church. His paralysed leg and arm began to 'swell considerably' and he was often 'seized with raving fits'. In September 1749, he made his final journey to Caldas and, when he returned to Lisbon on 6 October, he was, as the British envoy put it, 'in a deeper melancholy now than at any other time, for he has long entertained the notion of dying before his sixtieth year complete, no prince of the house of Bragança having ever reached that age'.

Despite his forebodings, the king survived his sixtieth birthday on 22 October. He lingered on for another nine months and, as the hot weather arrived in the summer of 1750, he lay in his bedchamber, bloated with oedema, scarcely able to move. The room was filled with priests and friars who recited prayers and held sacred images, amongst them a Jesuit – Gabriel Malagrida – a man treated with reverence by the royal couple who believed him to be a saint and a prophet.

João V died on 31 July, 'after a lingering distemper accompanied with various and extraordinary symptoms'. The doctors conducted a post mortem. 'A large quantity of water was found in his head and breast,' explained the British envoy, 'which his physicians are taxed with having brought upon him by larger bleedings and other evacuations.'

The body was taken to the church of São Vicente de Fora for interment in the royal mausoleum. João's two sons, José and

Pedro, accompanied the coffin to the palace doors but did not follow the cortège. According to ancient custom, all members of the family confined themselves to their apartments for eight days after the death and saw no-one but their servants.

The king had been a long time dying but no plans had been made for the transfer of power. The court was 'thrown into disarray'. José, the new monarch, felt out of his depth. By mistake, he doubled the length of court mourning – ordering two years instead of one – and was horrified to learn that his mother had plans to retire to a convent. He pleaded with her until she agreed to stay in the palace and advise him on matters of government, the most important of which was the appointment of his secretaries of state.

2

Princess of Brazil

The new king is irresolute, extremely diffident of himself, and conscious that his education has been greatly neglected.
Abraham Castres, 3 July 1751

Maria's father was thirty-six years old when he came to the throne, 'of good stature, but inclined to corpulency, his features regular, his eye quick and lively, and with a habit of holding his mouth somewhat open'.[7] Her mother, Mariana, was 'very agreeable in her person', with 'dark, lively and piercing eyes'.[8] The British envoy found her 'lively and affable' at official audiences, replying cheerfully to compliments and engaging him in long conversations. Intelligent and spirited, she often complained of the dullness and monotony of the Portuguese court.

José was formally enthroned on a hot sunny day in September, his wife by his side. The ceremony was an acclamation, not a coronation (a ritual discontinued in the 16th century when a king lost his life – and the diadem – on a battlefield in Morocco), but it was still a magnificent ceremony. A pavilion had been erected in the Terreiro do Paço and, on the afternoon of 7 September, the square was a heaving mass of people, the harbour filled with boats. As José took the oath, the crowds roared '*Viva Rei*', trumpets sounded, bells pealed, and the artillery fired a twenty-one-gun salute.

Maria sat in a box to one side of the pavilion with her grandmother and sisters. Over the years, her parents had produced four daughters (and four miscarriages), but there had been no pregnancies since 1746 and the doctors were not encouraging. She was fifteen years old and, as she watched her parents take centre stage, she was acutely aware of her future role in life. Portugal had no Salic law to exclude women from the succession so, unless her mother gave birth to a boy child – which seemed unlikely – she too would inherit the crown, the first woman to rule the country.

Having grown up in a court described as 'very dull and ceremonious' – even the British envoy referred to the 'excessive tediousness' of royal etiquette – Maria was accustomed to the many formalities of palace life. Now, as heir to the throne, she had to play a more important role. Her first official audience as crown princess (with the hereditary title of Princess of Brazil) was on 10 August. This was a *beija-mão*, the kissing of hands, an intricate procedure of bows and genuflexions as members of the court kissed the outstretched hands of royalty. She attended more ceremonies during the next few weeks and, in early October, the family travelled to the convent-palace in Mafra.

José was unsettled by his new responsibilities. He felt the need for fresh air and exercise and he travelled to Mafra, 'partly to attend the festival of St Francis and partly for the sake of hunting the stag and wild boar in the royal park nearby'.

The new king and queen were passionate about hunting and the family soon began to spend more time in the countryside. In early January, the royal barges took them upriver to Salvaterra de Magos where they hunted for several weeks and 'led a very jovial life'. In the spring, they set out on the three-day journey to Vila Viçosa, close to the border with Spain. The summer months were spent in Belém where they indulged in shooting and falconry, with excursions to Mafra for more hunting.

Mariana was an excellent horsewoman, her face burnt dark from long hours in the saddle. She rode astride, wearing black leather breeches covered by an old skirt, and was skilled at shooting. There were accidents from time to time – broken fingers, a dislocated shoulder, an occasion when her shot missed a partridge and grazed her husband's temple – but nothing could restrain the royal couple from their favourite pursuit. At

Salvaterra, they 'hardly passed a day without being on horseback five, six, and often eight or ten hours, especially on days appointed for wild boar which occurred very frequently'.

José's other passion was music, particularly Italian opera. He played the violin 'with considerable execution' and planned to transform his opera into 'the most pre-eminent in Europe'. The palace in Lisbon had its own magnificent theatre ('built at immense expense, the finest of its size in Europe, the scenery surpassing anything ever seen of the kind')[9] and he gave orders for a grand opera house to be built in the city, as well as a theatre in the hunting lodge at Salvaterra.

The royal singers and musicians accompanied the king as he travelled to and from his country palaces, and productions were staged several times a week. All female roles were sung by castrati, for José – like his father – was a libertine and Mariana was 'excessively jealous'. She not only banned all women from the royal opera, she also banned her attendants from appearing in the king's presence and was said to have chosen the oldest and ugliest women at court to be her ladies-in-waiting.

Despite her efforts, José had several mistresses, including the young Marquesa de Távora. During an opera performance at court in June 1755, a visitor noticed that 'the young Marquesa de Távora was very well with the king; they did nothing but eye each other as much as they dared in the queen's presence'.[10] A few months later, a scurrilous story did the rounds of Lisbon. Mariana – so the story went – was standing on a balcony in Belém watching José mount his horse in the square below. When one of her courtiers praised the graceful manner in which the king rode on horseback, she turned to the old Marquis de Távora who was standing beside her. 'It is true the king rides well,' she said to him, 'but you must allow that he rides better when he is with your daughter-in-law.'[11]

In September 1752, José marked the second anniversary of his acclamation with a series of bullfights and operas in Lisbon, including performances by a renowned Italian castrato. 'The court,' wrote the British envoy, 'is entirely taken up with bull-feasts, concerts and opera, almost every day of the week.'

Three months later, Maria reached her eighteenth birthday, an occasion celebrated with a *beija-mão* in the palace. She had grown tall and slender, with sharply defined features and a warm smile, and she accepted compliments from foreign ministers and members of the court with gracious elegance. Despite a limited education – taught by Jesuit priests with no emphasis on state affairs – she was an accomplished young woman. She spoke and read French, the diplomatic language of the courts of Europe. She read Latin and studied religion and theology. She was taught to draw and paint by the best artists in the country. She studied singing with David Perez, the Italian music master, and she and her sisters were 'proficient on different instruments'.

Kind and affectionate, timid and shy, Maria suffered from bouts of melancholy and nervous agitation. She had inherited her grandfather's religiosity and, deeply in thrall to the church, she sometimes longed to enter a convent, to become a nun and spend her days in prayer. With childlike simplicity, her bedroom was 'strewn with books of devotion and saintly dolls of all sorts and sizes'.[12]

Her faith was strengthened in the summer of 1753 when she nearly died of a 'violent inflammatory fever'. She was taken ill on 29 June during an opera in the palace and, as her fever increased, so the doctors relieved her of blood. Finally, having been bled six times, she was 'found to be in such immediate danger that the papal nuncio was sent for in great haste to give her the apostolic blessing *in articulo mortis*'. At the same time, her mother ordered that a wooden statue of Jesus be brought from the Convent da Graça.

The statue, believed to have miraculous powers, was known as *Senhor dos Passos* (Lord of the Passion). It depicted Jesus in purple robes, crowned with thorns, and carrying an enormous cross on his shoulders, 'stooping under the weight till his body was bent almost double'.[13] The statue was carried to the palace 'in great pomp' and placed in Maria's bedroom. She had been lying there 'in a deplorable condition' for more than twenty-four hours but, early next morning, 'some of the worst symptoms began to remit'.

By 8 July – 'to universal joy' – Maria was 'considerably better'. The British envoy attributed her recovery to a German doctor who, 'discovering the nature of the distemper, proposed remedies as were proper for malignant fevers and saved the life of this most amiable princess'. Maria herself never doubted that *Senhor dos Passos* had saved her life.

The statue was carried back to the convent 'with the greatest pomp and solemnity' and, by the end of the month, the royal family had moved to their palace at Belém. And while Maria regained her strength during the hot weeks of summer, one of her father's ministers was tightening his grip on power.

Sebastião de Carvalho e Melo – the future Marquis de Pombal – was an imposing man, six feet tall with a long face and handsome features. Born in 1699 into a family of minor gentry, he achieved little during his early life until, at the age of forty, he was appointed Portuguese ambassador to London. Four years later, he was sent as special envoy to the court of Vienna, a position he held until he returned to Lisbon in 1749.

The British envoy referred to Carvalho's 'difficult, chicaning temper', but marriage to an Austrian aristocrat led him into the favour of José's Austrian-born mother. João V had never trusted Carvalho – calling him 'a man with a hairy heart' – but his widow had great influence over her son. It was she who advised José to appoint him secretary of state for foreign affairs, the most junior of his three ministers.

The new king was, as the envoy put it, 'irresolute, extremely diffident of himself, and conscious that his education has been greatly neglected'. Unprepared for power, José followed his mother's advice in the appointment of ministers but showed little interest in government, preferring to spend his time at the opera or in the hunting field. In October 1750, the envoy remarked that, although his ministers met with José every day, 'they are supposed to have little or no weight with him, which has given rise to many lampoons, some very insolent ones, several of which have been dropt even in the king's bedchamber and others stuck up against the gates of the palace'.

José was also nervous and easily-led, traits which Carvalho – a highly intelligent and capable administrator – soon began to exploit. 'The minister is indefatigable, active and expeditious,' wrote the French chargé d'affaires in the autumn of 1750. 'He has won the confidence of the king and, in all political matters, none has it more than he.'[14] Six months later, the British envoy wrote that Carvalho was 'gaining ground in the king's good graces' and, by the summer of 1751, there had been a subtle change in the balance of power. As the envoy wrote in July:

> His Majesty showed at the beginning of his reign a greater suspicion of than confidence in his ministers in the dispatch of business, but since the ministers, particularly Monsieur de Carvalho, found means to establish credit with him, matters have been carried on with uncommon expedition, the king having shown a remarkable docility and patience in dispatching what was laid before him, much greater than could be expected from a prince so little used to business.

The balance of power continued to shift. 'Since the minister has had his foot in the stirrup,' the envoy wrote in June 1753, 'matters are greatly changed to his advantage.' By February 1754, 'the queen mother has lost her influence over her son and greatly repents having saddled him with Monsieur de Carvalho'.

José's mother did not live to repent for long. Seventy years old, her health was deteriorating and she asked the Jesuit, Gabriel Malagrida, to prepare her for death. When her condition worsened in July, the British envoy described her symptoms in a dispatch to London. The first complaint, he wrote, 'was a suppression of the urine which, having lasted two days, was at length removed by proper remedies. It is feared that the real distemper is a dropsy in the breast.' By 12 August, 'several livid spots had appeared on her legs' and the German doctor told José that she was showing 'signs of inward mortification'.

Maria Ana died two days later, 'having preserved her senses till the last moment'. Her body was interred in a convent of German nuns which she had founded in the city; her heart was sent home to Austria ('where everyone who knows her is convinced it has always been'). José grieved at the loss of his mother; as he did after his father died, he took his family into the countryside to spend his time hunting, the envoy commenting a few months later that 'the king and court have been much out of town of late'.

The following September, the annual treasure fleet arrived in Lisbon: twenty-six ships from Rio de Janeiro, their cargoes stuffed with gold and diamonds; a ship from Macao carrying 'twenty million *cruzados* of gold in dust and bars and coins'; nineteen ships from Bahia with treasure worth two million *cruzados*; and three ships from Goa on which the old Marquis de Távora returned to Lisbon from a posting as Viceroy of India. The appointment had been made by João V and the marquis had sailed for Goa in February 1750, taking his wife and elder son with him and leaving his daughter-in-law in Lisbon to catch the eye of José – the crown prince even travelled to the quayside to bid them farewell.

3

Earthquake

In a quarter of an hour, this great city was laid in ruins.
Edward Hay, 15 November 1755

On 20 October 1755, the British envoy sent a dispatch to the secretary of state in London. 'We have nothing stirring here,' he wrote, 'that deserves His Majesty's attention.'

Twelve days later, the morning of 1 November was unseasonably warm, the sun shining from a cloudless sky. The people were in church to celebrate mass for All Saints' Day when, at half-past nine, they heard a noise which sounded like the king's heavy carriage rattling through the streets. The earth shuddered, then jerked upwards in a motion that felt like a wagon being driven violently over rough stones. The captain of a ship in the harbour watched the buildings of Lisbon rock to and fro like corn in the wind before they began to crumble in vast clouds of dust. 'In a quarter of an hour,' wrote the British consul, 'this great city was laid in ruins.'

When the dust began to clear, swarms of people could be seen stumbling amongst the piles of shattered stonework:

> Old, young, male and female, seeking their parents, children, relations and friends, many sick, many maimed from the fall of houses, some dead and most half naked, so dismal a sight as was never seen ... friars and priests giving absolution, confessing and praying with everyone; the coaches and chaises, horses and mules, buried under the ground; people under the ruins begging for assistance and none able to get near them; old people, hardly able to walk, without shoes and stockings.[15]

Able-bodied survivors clambered over the ruins, heading for the river bank where they would be safe from collapsing buildings. But soon the waters in the Tagus receded, followed by the sight of a giant wave moving towards the city. 'Turning my eyes towards the river,' wrote an English merchant:

> I perceived it heaving and swelling in a most unaccountable manner. In an instant, there appeared a vast body of water, rising like a mountain. It came on foaming and roaring, and rushed towards the shore with such impetuosity that, although we all ran for our lives, many were swept away.[16]

Three tsunamis surged up the Tagus that morning. Ships were ripped from their anchors and crashed into each other, the waves inundating the low-lying areas of the city. They tore at buildings on the river banks, swept away the marble-faced quay in the Terreiro do Paço, and destroyed everything in their path.

Aftershocks continued throughout the morning and, by early afternoon, most of the city was in flames. The fall of curtains and woodwork onto candles lit for All Saints' Day in every church and chapel led to the outbreak of numerous fires which soon joined into one vast conflagration. People fled to the suburbs, clambering over the ruins, their way littered with the dead and the dying:

> In some places lay coaches, with their masters, horses and riders almost crushed in pieces. Here were mothers with infants in their arms, there ladies richly dressed. Priests, friars, gentlemen, mechanics, some with their backs or thighs broken, others with vast stones on their breasts. Some lay almost buried in the rubbish and, crying out in vain for succour, were left to perish with the rest.[17]

By evening, the open spaces around Belém were filled with crowds of confused and frightened people. And as it grew dark, 'the whole city appeared in a blaze so bright ... the people had their eyes turned towards the flames and stood looking on with silent grief, interrupted by the shrieks of women and children whenever the earth began to tremble, which was so often this night that the tremors did not cease for a quarter of an hour together'.[18]

The royal family, in their palace at Belém, were not yet dressed for the day when the earth began to rumble and shake. José jumped out of a ground-floor window at the first jolt, followed a few minutes later by his wife and daughters, still in their night-clothes and wrapped in bed sheets.

During the hours which followed, servants bustled about the gardens erecting tents for their accommodation, while Maria gazed eastwards along the Tagus to the dust cloud that hung over the ruins of Lisbon. She watched the waters rising and receding as the giant waves surged up the river and, when dark fell in the evening, the fires in the city lit up the sky. That night, she lay in her tent in the palace gardens. She felt the earth continue to tremble, she heard the cries of the refugees in Belém. It was difficult to sleep through the long hours of darkness, but 'long-wished-for day at last appeared and the sun rose with great splendour on the desolated city in the morning'.[19]

It was another bright, sunny day. The fires were still burning. Fanned by a north-east wind, they burned for another five days and it was some time before the people of Lisbon could return to the city and move with difficulty through the rubble. 'It is not to be expressed by human tongue,' wrote the captain of a ship who ventured ashore:

> how dreadful and awful it was to enter the city after the fire was abated. Looking upwards, one was struck with terror in beholding pyramids of ruined fronts, some inclining one way, some another. Then one was struck with horror in beholding dead bodies, six or seven in a heap, crushed to death, half buried and half burnt, and nothing to be met with but people bewailing their misfortunes, wringing their hands and crying *misericordia*, the world is at an end.[20]

José was overwhelmed by the disaster. When Carvalho (whose house in the Bairro Alto remained intact) arrived in Belém a few hours after the earthquake, he had found the king surrounded by priests and in a state of total bewilderment.

'What is to be done?' José asked him.

'Bury the dead,' replied Carvalho, 'and feed the living.'

Given full powers to restore order, the future Marquis de Pombal lived in his carriage for eight days. He wrote more than two hundred proclamations and encouraged people to dig for survivors and provide food and shelter for the homeless. For one period of twenty-four hours, he ate nothing but a bowl of soup brought by his wife who picked her way over the ruins to his carriage.

Corpses were collected in barges, towed out to sea and thrown overboard. Looters were hanged, their bodies left exposed as a deterrent to others. Incoming vessels with shipments of fish, corn and meat were compelled to sell their cargoes; outgoing vessels were searched for stolen treasure. Paths were made through the ruins, depots requisitioned and food centres organised. Shelters were erected in open spaces, latrines dug, and temporary hospitals set up for the wounded and destitute.

Meanwhile, the royal family were made as comfortable as possible in the tents at Belém, although it took a few days to organise their furniture and furnishings, their clothing and articles of toilette. On 5 November, when the British envoy came to offer his condolences, José received him 'with more serenity than I expected, while the queen and princesses sent word that, being in their tents and in a dress not fit to appear in, they desired that I would excuse their accepting my compliments in person'.

Maria re-emerged in public on 16 November when she and her family walked barefoot in a 'solemn penitential procession' led by the Patriarch in the suburbs west of the city. Aftershocks continued to jolt the earth, sometimes with violence, and her twenty-first birthday on 17 December went largely unheeded. Five days later, she attended an official audience in what had become known as the 'royal tent' as her father thanked the British envoy for his government's swift response to the disaster.

Ships had been sent from England laden with money in gold coins, foodstuffs, shoes and clothing, picks, shovels and crowbars, and José's thanks were expressed in the usual effusive language. In a letter written to London on 24 December, the envoy wrote that the king and queen had spoken with 'a mixture of complacency and tenderness, both in their looks and tone of voice, and plainly showed the emotion of their hearts'.

Tens of thousands of people had died, crushed by falling masonry, drowned in the tsunamis, burnt in the flames. The palace in the Terreiro do Paço was in ruins, together with José's new opera house, the patriarchal church, convents and nunneries, churches and chapels, thousands of shops and houses. Maria and her sisters prepared lint and bandages for the wounded, while servants raked through the debris of the palace. By early January, they had found most of the royal diamonds, together with twenty-two tons of melted silver plate, and Maria was delighted to learn that *Senhor dos Passos* had been rescued unharmed from the ruins of the Convent da Graça.

Belém, three miles from the area of greatest devastation, had suffered little damage. The palace was structurally sound but José insisted that his family remain in tents while a new palace, built of wood, was constructed on the nearby hill of Ajuda. 'The terrors of the earthquake were so deeply impressed on his mind,' explained a visitor to Lisbon, 'that he preferred to reside in wooden or tented buildings, however mean or inconvenient, rather than encounter the perils attached to a stone edifice.'[21]

The royal tents were cold during the winter months and rain leaked through the canvas seams. Maria was unaccustomed to such discomfort, although her servants did their best to provide warmth and luxury. They brought her collection of 'saintly dolls' from the palace, they lined the tent with rugs and tapestries, they kept the braziers burning and piled up her bed with coverings. Troubled that so many people had died while celebrating mass for All Saints' Day, she was comforted by her Jesuit confessor who assured her that the disaster was God's punishment for their sins.

Meanwhile, in the open spaces around Belém, thousands of homeless people were living in makeshift shelters of wood and canvas. Business was at a standstill, food was in short supply, and because so many churches had been destroyed, priests were hearing confessions and conducting services in the open air.

In January 1757, the royal family left Belém for the first time since the earthquake, setting out on the thirty-mile journey upriver to Salvaterra de Magos. As the royal barge passed the waterfront of the city, Maria gazed at the toppled churches and convents, the ruins of the royal palace, the rubble heaped up in the Terreiro do Paço. 'Nothing is to be seen,' wrote Joseph Baretti who arrived on a packet boat from Falmouth, 'but vast heaps of rubbish, out of which arise the miserable remains of shattered walls and broken pillars.'[22]

The family enjoyed the hunting in Salvaterra and returned to Belém in March. Four months later, the new wooden palace was ready for occupation. This was the *Barraca Real* (the royal hut), a long single-storey building described by a jaundiced observer as 'a very mean structure, with no kind of magnificence'.[23] And as Maria settled into her new home, an Englishman – William Stephens – opened a lime factory in the suburb of Alcântara, a mile from Belém on the Lisbon road.

Intended to provide mortar for rebuilding the city, his kilns were built to a modern, industrial design, unlike anything ever seen in Portugal. From the windows of the palace, Maria watched the smoke rising from the chimneys and, when she was driven past the factory gates, she sometimes saw Stephens standing in the courtyard as he stopped work to watch the royal carriages pass by.

4

The Rise of Pombal

The minister has the entire management of the affairs of this kingdom. He carries a high hand and makes all ranks of people stand in awe of him.
Edward Hay, 1 March 1766

The fact that Pombal's house was undamaged in the earthquake was a sign – in José's opinion – of divine guidance, proof that the minister had been sent by God to help him in his hour of need. His influence with the king was greatly enhanced by this stroke of luck, as well as by his efficient handling of the disaster, and in May 1756, he was appointed the most senior secretary of state, with the portfolio for home affairs. As the British consul put it, 'Monsieur de Carvalho is now the leading man, and is in effect prime minister, for nothing is done without him'.

Pombal viewed the earthquake as a natural event, but his plans to restore order were hampered by the clergy who insisted that the disaster was a punishment from God. As the first anniversary approached, the Jesuit – Gabriel Malagrida – published a pamphlet attacking Pombal's policies and thundering on about divine retribution:

> Learn, O Lisbon, that the destroyer of our houses, palaces, churches and convents, the reason for the deaths of so many people and the flames that devoured such vast quantities of treasure, are your own abominable sins. It is scandalous to pretend the earthquake was just a natural event for, if that be true, there is no need to repent and try to avert the wrath of God. It is necessary to devote all our strength to the task of repentance. God is watching us, scourge in hand.[24]

Pombal, who had worked so hard to restore order in the city, was furious. He accused the Jesuits of using the disaster to 'frighten feeble and superstitious minds'. He persuaded the papal nuncio to banish Malagrida to Setúbal (twenty miles south of Lisbon) and drafted an edict denouncing the pamphlet as 'fanatical, malicious and heretical'. Meanwhile, several Jesuits had begun to plot against him, their intrigues mirrored at court where the nobles also simmered with resentment, having lost much of their power and influence over the king.

Pombal showed his teeth for the first time in the summer of 1756 when he arranged the disgrace of Diogo de Mendonça, one of his fellow secretaries of state. Mendonça was jealous of Pombal; he was indiscreet enough to criticise him at dinner parties and there was talk of a conspiracy. On 31 August, he was banished from Lisbon and given three hours to leave the city. Within a few months, he had been arrested, imprisoned and exiled to Angola. And like so many of those banished to the African colony, he died there from the effects of extreme climate, disease and malnutrition.

Mendonça was not alone in his disgrace. Having convinced himself that Jesuits were involved in the conspiracy, Pombal persuaded José to dismiss all Jesuit confessors from the *Barraca Real*. Ordered to return to the colleges of their order, they left the palace on 19 September and Maria lost her confessor, Timoteo de Oliveira, a man she held in great respect. In June 1758, the Society of Jesus was ordered to cease all business affairs and banned from preaching and taking confessions. Pombal's excuse for these measures was that Jesuits had been plotting against the government in South America but, as the British envoy noted, 'the order of Jesuits is very powerful in this country and their disgrace is the more remarkable'.

José was complicit in these actions against the Jesuits; he signed the edicts that Pombal placed before him. The French ambassador reported that the king was showing signs of nervous tension in the summer of 1758, perhaps concerned that his minister was going too far. He appeared, wrote the ambassador 'weak and anxious, as if anticipating some great calamity.'[25]

On 31 August, a letter arrived from Madrid informing José of the death of his sister Bárbara (wife of Ferdinand VI of Spain). According to custom, he ordered his family to confine themselves to their apartments for eight days and imposed a court mourning of six months. 'Unhappily,' wrote the British envoy on 13 September, 'the execution of this order has been interrupted by His Majesty's indisposition, it being the custom of this court to put on gala when any of the royal family is blooded.'

The king had been bled by the doctors. It was given out that he had fallen in the *Barraca Real* on the night of 3 September and bruised his arm, and since he was advised to 'refrain from business for some time', his wife was acting as regent during his indisposition.

José should have been confined to his rooms during the evening of 3 September, grieving for his sister, but the truth was that he had slipped out of the palace to visit his mistress, the young Marquesa de Távora. It was a dark night – the second night of a new moon – and on the return journey shortly before midnight, while his chaise was passing down a narrow lane, three masked horsemen emerged from the darkness and opened fire. The first shot misfired, the second and third ripped into the back of the chaise. José was not seriously wounded – shot had grazed his shoulder and arm – and as the horsemen galloped away into the darkness, he told his coachman to drive direct to the royal surgeon's house in the Rua da Junqueira.

His wounds dressed, the king returned to Belém and sent a messenger for Pombal to come to the palace. Next morning, on Pombal's advice, the story about the fall was given out. Rumours spread around the city and, on 13 September, the British envoy explained that the assassination attempt had 'greatly alarmed the court, where it is endeavoured to be hushed up, but it is talked of abroad more publicly than prudently. What a condition this unhappy nation would have been in had the king fallen.'

Maria was horrified when she learned the truth – but Pombal sensed an opportunity. His ambitions were to increase the commercial prosperity of the country and (as he told the envoy) to 'emancipate the nation from subjection to the See of Rome and eradicate old prejudices from the minds of a superstitious people'. But he also had a despotic side to his nature and was certainly a man to hold grudges. In his youth, he had proposed marriage to a daughter of the Távora family and the Távoras, sneering at his provincial background, had ordered him out of their house. The Duke de Aveiro, too, had become an enemy. The most important nobleman in Portugal, he had never concealed his dislike of Pombal. It was he who headed the opposition to the indolent manner in which José ran his country – and to Pombal as the king's first minister.

During the next three months, Pombal used his spies to collect 'evidence' against the aristocrats and their Jesuit confessors. The suspects were arrested on 13 December. They included the Duke de Aveiro and all the Távora family: the old marquis; his wife, the old marquesa; his four brothers; his two sons (the elder of whom – the young marquis – was the husband of José's mistress); and his two sons-in-law (Count de Atouguia and Marquis de Alorna). Also arrested were thirteen Jesuit priests, including Gabriel Malagrida (who had been acting as spiritual guide to the old marquesa) and Timoteo de Oliveira (Maria's confessor until his recent dismissal).

Pombal persuaded José to allow the use of torture, presiding over the proceedings as fifty prisoners were interrogated on the rack. Servants were tortured to extract information about their employers, nobles tortured into betraying their friends. The trials began on 9 January and the verdicts – a foregone conclusion – were announced three days later. The defendants were found guilty of treason, ten of them to be executed the following day in Belém.

Six of the condemned were aristocrats and Maria knew them well. It was said that she pleaded with her father when the sentences were announced but José was unmoved by her tears. All night, the carpenters worked on the scaffold, fixing six wheels onto the platform, one for each of the nobles. And lying in her bed in the *Barraca Real*, Maria heard the distant sounds as they sawed and hammered through the night.

In the morning, a light rain was falling as the condemned arrived at the scaffold one by one. The old marquesa came first. She was beheaded. Next came her two sons and one of her sons-in-law (Atouguia). They were each tied to a wheel, their ribs, legs and arms broken with hammers before a garrotte put an end to their lives. Their corpses lay exposed on the wheels when the Duke de Aveiro and the old marquis mounted the scaffold to suffer the same treatment. Finally, one of the 'assassins' was burnt alive and the whole platform set alight, the mangled bodies burnt to ashes.

The following day, Maria attended an official audience in the *Barraca Real* to receive compliments on her father's escape from death. On 15 January, she accompanied her family to the church of Nossa Senhora do Livramento in Alcântara, where the *Te Deum* was sung to celebrate the execution of the king's enemies. It was the first time José had appeared in public since the assassination attempt and he waved his handkerchief in the air with both hands, one after the other, to show the crowd that he had suffered no lasting injury.

During the next three days, the king and his family attended a religious festival (the Devotion of Santa Engracia) and, on 19 January, they left Belém to spend six weeks in Salvaterra. Two years earlier, as the royal barge was rowed up the Tagus, Maria had seen the ruins of Lisbon spread out behind the waterfront; now it seemed that a reign of terror had begun. 'There is not the least outward demonstration of discontent,' explained the British envoy, 'but much inward murmurings and heart-burnings at the measures of a certain great minister.'

As a final mark of disgrace, the houses of the Távora and Aveiro families were demolished, the sites sprinkled with salt so that nothing more would grow there.

Having cowed the aristocracy, Pombal continued his campaign against the Jesuits. In July, they were 'deprived of their schools and colleges'. A few weeks later, on the first anniversary of his escape from the gunmen, José signed an edict banishing all Jesuit priests from Portugal and its colonies. In the words of the edict (no doubt drafted by Pombal), they were referred to as 'notorious rebels, traitors, enemies and aggressors against the royal person of the king, against the public peace of this kingdom, and against the common good of his subjects'. And as such, they were 'outlawed, proscribed and exterminated for ever out of the kingdom and dominions of Portugal'.

Nine years earlier, when José came to the throne, the country was ruled by the monarch, the church and the aristocracy. Now the nobility and the church had both been crushed and Pombal was – in effect – dictator of the country. The dungeons were filled with people suspected of further intrigues, men and women arrested and imprisoned without trial. Nobody dared discuss politics or criticise Pombal's actions; it was illegal even to speak of the Távora conspiracy. 'So many have been thrown into jail on this account,' wrote a visitor to Lisbon, 'that the poor souls are quite frighted at the mention of some names.'[26]

5

A Quiet Wedding

How long and how ardently the nobility, the whole people of this kingdom, have sighed for this event.
Lord Kinnoull, 7 June 1760

Maria celebrated her twenty-fifth birthday with a *beija-mão* in Ajuda, aware that her father had abdicated responsibility for his country. José attended few meetings of state, rarely gave audiences to foreign ministers and, placing full authority in Pombal's hands, simply signed the documents that were put before him, often in the early hours of the morning after he had spent his days on horseback and his evenings at the opera.

Writers of the time refer to her expression of melancholy and it was public knowledge that Maria's mind was 'deeply impressed with the tragic catastrophe of the Duke de Aveiro and his associates, whose fate she lamented as unmerited and unjust'.[27] She loathed Pombal for his persecution of the church as well as for his tyranny. She tried to believe that José had acted fairly but her instincts told her that the minister – and by default her father also – had persecuted God's representatives on earth.

Twenty-five was a late age for a princess in the marriage market. Maria's mother had married at the age of ten, her aunt Bárbara at seventeen, but this was the first time that a female was heir to the throne of Portugal. As the British envoy explained, 'the succession is a most tender point and attended with circumstances of equal difficulty and importance'. Under the fundamental laws of the country (the 12th-century Laws of Lamego), Maria was forbidden to marry a foreign prince:

> If the king have no male issue and have a daughter, she shall be queen after the death of the king provided that she marry a Portuguese nobleman. The law shall always be observed that the eldest daughter of the king shall have no other husband than a Portuguese lord in order that foreign princes may not become masters of the kingdom. If the king's daughter marries a foreign prince or noble, she shall not be recognised as queen.[28]

Despite these laws, there had been several half-hearted attempts to arrange a betrothal with a foreign prince, including the Duke of Cumberland (third son of George II) and one of Maria's uncles in Spain. These came to nothing, as did an early attraction between Maria and João de Bragança, her father's first cousin. The laws about the marriage of a crown princess had never been tested and it was feared that, if Maria married into the Portuguese aristocracy, the succession would be disputed by male members of the Bragança family.

Her grandfather proposed a solution as early as 1749. He suggested that she marry her uncle Pedro, her father's younger brother, but Mariana opposed the idea. Pedro was 'suspected to have great sway over his brother' and, fearing that he was ambitious for power, she brought José round to her point of view. At the same time, Pedro's enemies spread rumours that he was impotent, that he suffered from 'some natural defect which will not allow him to become the Princess of Brazil's husband and will oblige him, in all likelihood, to enter into holy orders'.

Pombal also viewed Pedro with suspicion. On one occasion, he persuaded José to banish him to his country house at Queluz (a few miles west of Lisbon) on the pretext that he was planning a coup against him, but Maria soon persuaded her father to revoke the order. It was true that Pedro disliked Pombal, but he was harmless enough and he soon lost his more youthful ambition. The rumours of impotence died away, people continued to talk of the marriage (in 1754, it was 'impatiently expected by people of all ranks') and, by the spring of 1760, José and Mariana had changed their minds.

Pedro was eighteen years older than Maria, a simple man with no interest in state affairs. Like his niece, he was deeply devout, 'constantly engaged in prayers and processions'.[29] He was rebuilding his house at Queluz and it would soon be converted into a miniature Versailles, a rococo palace surrounded by formal gardens, citrus groves, water cascades and fountains.

There were lavish entertainments at Queluz during the summer months, private parties restricted to members of the royal family and their ladies- and gentlemen-in-waiting. The fêtes on 24 and 29 June (the feast days of São João and São Pedro) were particularly elaborate, with horse races, bullfights, banquets, and concerts in the music room where the queen and her daughters sang. As it grew dark, the gardens were lit by thousands of wax tapers, shifting illuminations moved over the façade of the palace, and fireworks burst into the night sky.

On the morning of 6 June 1760, the British envoy attended the *Barraca Real* for an audience in honour of the king's birthday:

> which happened upon so extraordinary a day, when the court was so agreeably surprised with a most welcome declaration of His Majesty's intentions, that a marriage should be *that* evening celebrated between his brother, the Infante Dom Pedro, and his daughter, the Princess of Brazil. I need not mention how long and how ardently the nobility, the whole people of this kingdom, have sighed for this interesting event, or the great and universal joy with which the almost unexpected accomplishment of their wishes was received.

It was a quiet wedding by royal standards, celebrated privately in the chapel of the *Barraca Real*. Five years after the losses sustained in the earthquake, Maria's father was ensuring that 'the nobility and gentry are put to no expense'. He was aware of the cost of his own marriage in 1729 and now, 'through His Majesty's paternal attention, things have been so managed that there will not be so much as the additional expense of a suit of clothes'.

Three days of public rejoicings were ordered as soon as the ceremony had taken place. Bells rang, cannons fired, and the people placed lighted candles in their windows. And that night, according to ancient ritual, Maria's mother and sisters prepared her for the marriage bed. They undressed her, perfumed her body, laid her between fine linen sheets, and waited until Pedro entered the chamber and climbed in beside her.

Maria delighted in marriage. She enjoyed her husband's warm body and on her wedding night (following her grandfather's example) she vowed to build a church and convent dedicated to the Heart of Jesus – to which she was 'especially devoted' – if she was blessed with the birth of a son. Members of the court commented on her radiant smile but Pombal soon cast his shadow over her first weeks of conjugal bliss.

First, he banished the papal nuncio from the country. He had been trying to break off relations with the Vatican for some time, accusing the nuncio of 'intermeddling with His Majesty's government and fermenting a dangerous sedition amongst the king's subjects'. Now he had an excuse. The nuncio had failed to illuminate his house in celebration of the marriage and Pombal chose to perceive this as an insult to the royal family. On 14 June, in the nuncio's own words:

> An order was brought to me to quit Lisbon within the hour but the fifty soldiers who brought the order did not allow me a minute. Their commander hurried me into a boat without giving me time to shut my writing-desk, took me across the Tagus and saw me to the river Caya in four days. On the road, I had no bed and scarce anything to eat, and all this without my knowing why.[30]

'This step,' wrote the British envoy, 'has stunned and astonished many who never thought to have seen such a measure taken in Portugal.'

Six days after the nuncio's departure, Pombal arrested and imprisoned two senior members of the aristocracy, Count de São Lourenço and Viscount de Vila Nova da Cerveira, both accused of intriguing with the nuncio, although their real crime was being a little too free in their conversation. Vila Nova had acted as ambassador in Madrid for seven years and was, according to the envoy, 'a man of outstanding experience, honour and integrity'. São Lourenço was a friend of Pedro and was known as a wit. When it was said that Pombal's house had been saved from the earthquake by divine providence, he made the point that God had also preserved the Rua Suja – the street of brothels – a joke the minister did not appreciate.

Finally, on 21 July, Pombal disgraced two of Maria's uncles (bastard sons of João V), banishing them to a convent in the hills of Buçaco. José had elevated his half-brothers to the rank of princes of royal blood but Pombal now accused them of corresponding with the nuncio and being 'deeply engaged in all his intrigues'. It was said that one of the princes, hoping to marry Maria and disappointed at her marriage to Pedro, had taken to 'caballing' with the nuncio and the Jesuits. A more likely explanation is the story of an argument between Pombal and the princes, which ended with one of them pulling off the minister's wig and 'beating it about his face'.[31]

Pedro's parties were even more magnificent after his marriage and on 29 June – as an exceptional honour – the British envoy was led through the gardens of Queluz to enjoy the festivities for São Pedro's day. He watched a bullfight and a concert by the royal musicians, enjoyed a banquet in a marquee, and was in the audience when Mariana and her daughters sang. He noted his impressions carefully:

> The queen, who is a superior mistress of music, sings with that perfect skill and knowledge which conceals every defect of the voice and always gives delight. The princesses, taught by David Perez, the best master in Europe, all discover a most excellent taste. The second, Mariana, both in voice and execution may be ranked with the very best performers and the youngest, Benedita, whose person is extremely beautiful and agreeable, sings charmingly.

'The whole of this entertainment,' he concluded, 'was the most princely and magnificent that I ever saw and the serenity of the night did justice to the splendour of it.'

Every Sunday afternoon in summer, the king and his family sat in state to watch the bullfights in the wooden bullring at Campo Pequeno. Joseph Baretti was in the audience on 31 August and he saw them take their seats in the royal box. José, he wrote, 'was dressed in plain sky blue with some diamonds about him'; Mariana and her daughters were 'sparkling with jewels'.

Towards the end of the afternoon, as the eighth bull was being dragged from the arena, a group of pickpockets leapt over the barriers, shouting '*Terremoto*! *Terremoto*!' ('Earthquake! Earthquake!'), shouts which terrified the spectators. Maria and her sisters 'raised their hands, fans and voices, as I could see by the opening of their mouths', while the audience 'leapt precipitously into the arena with the most hideous shrieks and ran about like madmen'. The pickpockets did good business that afternoon, 'many men lost their handkerchiefs and many women their caps, not to speak of swords and watches, necklaces and ear-rings'.[32]

Three days later, Baretti attended a ceremony in Belém on the second anniversary of the assassination attempt. A pavilion had been built on the exact spot, the interior 'hung with red serge striped and fringed with tinsel-lace', the altar in the centre 'gloriously adorned' with gold and silver candlesticks. And during a lavish ceremony orchestrated by Pombal, José laid the foundation stone of a memorial church to commemorate his escape from the gunmen.

Pombal arrived first with his bodyguard of forty men on horseback who followed his carriage with their swords drawn, 'an officer with a drummer attending him and beating at their head'. Then came the Patriarch and his establishment in a train of forty coaches, followed by the royal family in carriages drawn by six piebald horses. 'The princesses were most magnificently dressed,' wrote Baretti, 'wearing ample hoops, their heads, necks, breasts, arms, waists and feet glittering with jewels.

They appeared so lively, hopping out of the coach with so much nimbleness.'

It was a hot day and the windows of the pavilion were thrown open, giving Baretti a clear view of the proceedings. As Maria and her sisters knelt to pray, their mother began a furious bout of kissing the pages of her prayer book, 'more than forty times in a few minutes'. The *Te Deum* was sung – 'with much noise of music' – then José, Pedro and Pombal left their seats. They descended into a hole in the floor where 'silver shovels, silver hammers and other implements of masonry had been placed with stones, bricks and mortar'.

José placed some gold and silver coins on the earth at the bottom of the hole. He covered the coins with a stone, after which the three men 'took up their shovels and fell a-covering the stone with bricks and mortar, beating the bricks with hammers as directed by the architect. Some women looking through the windows laughed immoderately at the masons because they were somewhat awkward at their new trade, and this discomposed a little the gravity of the bystanders.'

To stifled laughter from the crowd, José, Pedro and Pombal left the hole and returned to their seats. The Patriarch celebrated mass and the royal musicians 'played and sang most gloriously'.[33]

6

Nuptial Felicity

In all the duties and departments of private life,
she was exemplary ... a model of nuptial felicity.
Sir William Wraxall, 1772

After their marriage, Maria and Pedro appeared side-by-side at official audiences but took no part in state affairs. They confined themselves to religion and family life, while Pombal continued his vendetta against the church, the country was embroiled in the final stages of the Seven Years' War, and José was attacked for a second time in the hunting park at Vila Viçosa.

Maria conceived eight children in fifteen years. Two were late miscarriages, three died in infancy, and three survived to adulthood. Her first child was born in the *Barraca Real* shortly before midnight on 20 August 1761, in a room filled with priests, secretaries of state, courtiers and attendants. This was the son she had prayed for; she named him José after her father and the city celebrated with peals of bells, cannon-fire and illuminations.

The infant prince was baptised in the palace chapel seven days later, but Maria did not reappear in public until 24 September when she attended a bullfight in honour of her newborn son. Her happiness on this occasion was tarnished by the knowledge that Gabriel Malagrida, the priest whom her grandparents had revered as a saint and a prophet, had been garrotted and burnt at the stake four days earlier in the main square of Lisbon.

Malagrida was the best-known Jesuit in Portugal, reason enough for Pombal to hate him; his pamphlet about the earthquake had only added to the minister's desire for revenge. Old and tired, and almost certainly out of his mind, Malagrida had languished in dungeons for more than two years until Pombal found a way to be rid of him. He handed him over to the Inquisition and personally drew up the indictment: heresy, blasphemy, false prophecy, and 'having abused the Word of God'.

The *auto-da-fé* on the night of 20 September was attended by Maria's father and husband and all the court. Thousands of people gathered in the square and, as they watched the garrotte tighten around the old priest's throat, as they watched the faggots burning, press-gangs moved amongst them to seize young men for service in the army. The war in Europe was threatening to become a wider conflict. Portuguese neutrality was in danger – an alliance between France and Spain having opened the door to invasion – and the country's defences were in an appalling state, 'totally neglected, sunk into the most wretched condition'.

In March 1762, the French and Spanish governments 'demanded to know' whether Portugal was willing to renounce the Anglo-Portuguese alliance and close its ports to British shipping. In early May, after José refused these demands, Franco-Spanish forces crossed the northern border. Pombal called on the old alliance and Britain sent eight thousand troops to Lisbon. They arrived in June and, before marching north to engage the enemy, the officers were invited to the entertainments at Queluz. They were led through the gardens (as the British envoy had been two years before) and, after watching a bullfight and eating 'an elegant supper', the senior officers were ushered into the music room to hear the queen and princesses sing.

Skirmishes were fought during the next few months but the war in Europe was coming to an end. The invading army retreated in October and a general ceasefire was declared a few weeks later. Now, at last, Pombal could turn his mind to a project close to his heart, the rebuilding of Lisbon.

He had first discussed his ideas for a modern city to rise from the ruins a few weeks after the earthquake, a city of wide streets built on a grid system with raised pedestrian pavements and a good sewage system. To enable the work to be carried out quickly and cheaply, the design was a simple one, a style of plain-fronted buildings with wrought iron balconies (which became known as Pombaline). He had intended the work to start as early as 1757 but, mainly because of the preparations for war, it was delayed for seven years while the city remained in heaps of rubble.

The reconstruction finally began during the long hot summer of 1764. Builders set to work in the low-lying area near the Terreiro do Paço, but rebuilding the royal palace was not one of Pombal's priorities. Instead, the square was renamed Praça do Comércio and lined with commercial and military buildings.

Maria miscarried her second child in October 1762, in the sixth month of pregnancy. The following September, she gave birth to a boy who lived for just three weeks, 'a loss she handled with surprising fortitude and resignation'. She produced a healthy son (Prince João) in May 1767 and conceived again ten months later.

Her fifth pregnancy had almost reached full term when, on 8 December 1768, she attended a performance of Molière's *Tartuffe* in a theatre in Lisbon. The play was about religious hypocrisy. Tartuffe, the arch-hypocrite, puts on a display of fake piety to ingratiate himself with a wealthy bourgeois, then swindles him out of his money and his wife. The title role was played in Jesuit costume. The audience had no difficulty in recognising the subtext of the production and three people were 'committed to prison for speaking their sentiments too freely on the subject of this new play'.

The following day, Pombal ordered the arrest of one of Maria's favourite clerics. The elderly Bishop of Coimbra, Miguel da Anunciação, was related to the Távora family, a man described by the British envoy as 'a morose, stubborn, hot-headed bigot'. His crime was to write a pastoral letter condemning several books which had been specifically sanctioned by the Real Mesa Censória (a secular body set up by Pombal to take over matters of censorship from the Inquisition). The bishop was sentenced to death for treason – 'for a long train of projects designed to counteract and subvert His Majesty's government' – but, in view of his age, he was spared execution. Instead, he was brought to Lisbon under military guard and imprisoned in a fort at the mouth of the Tagus.

Six days after the bishop's arrest, Maria gave birth to her fourth child, a daughter named Mariana. On 23 December, copies of the offending letter (which, according to Pombal, had 'almost certainly been dictated from Rome') were burnt by the public executioner 'as false, seditious and treasonable', and Pombal told the British envoy that he had been given full authority 'to take all such measures as might silence the machinations of turbulent ecclesiastics'.

'How formidable an ecclesiastical faction is to any country,' ruminated the envoy in a dispatch to London. 'The steadiness of the king's favour, and the vigour with which the minister enters into all his measures, will perhaps enable him to subdue the ecclesiastical hydra, although new heads should spring up in proportion as others are lopped off.'

José may have allowed Pombal to persecute the clergy but his conscience was troubled by the break with the Vatican. As he celebrated his fifty-fifth birthday in June 1769, he was aware that his father had suffered a near-fatal stroke at the earlier age of fifty-two. He had no wish to die without papal absolution so, to humour him, Pombal re-established relations with Rome. The breach had lasted ten years, long enough for Pombal to remove the church's dominance over national affairs. He had created a secular state, placed the church under government control, and reduced the powers of the Inquisition. As the British envoy noted, 'although it was resolved to re-admit the lion, it was with his nails cut and his teeth drawn'.

A new papal nuncio was appointed in August and, on 16 September, José thanked his minister by giving him the title by which he is known to history: Marquis de Pombal. Five weeks later, the royal family left Lisbon for an extended stay in Vila Viçosa. They went hunting every day and, on the morning of 3 December, the king set out for the chase ahead of his attendants.

He was passing through a gate into the walled hunting park when a 'tall strong man in the habit of a peasant' attacked him with a wooden pole, 'a long staff with one end knottier and heavier than the other end which formed the handle'.

The man, a muleteer named João de Sousa, aimed three blows at the king: the first hit his shoulder, the second landed on his left hand, the third hit his horse behind the saddle. The royal attendants galloped to the rescue, but Sousa fought with great strength and managed to wound two of them before he was finally overpowered. José, who only suffered bruises to his hand and shoulder, continued the hunt; Sousa was taken off to the dungeons.

That afternoon, the palace was in turmoil. Mariana was aghast at how close she had come, yet again, to losing her husband; Maria was terrified at the prospect of inheriting the throne so suddenly, a position for which she was painfully unprepared. An urgent message was sent to Pombal in Lisbon who dispatched two magistrates to interrogate the prisoner.

Sousa had a grievance against the king. His mules had been requisitioned for the journey of the court to Vila Viçosa and one of them was driven so hard that it died on the road. He had petitioned José for compensation but his request was ignored. He was ill-treated, angry and, it was said, 'partially out of his wits'. But Pombal chose to blame the Society of Jesus. The attack, he said, was a Jesuit conspiracy, a suicide mission; the muleteer had fought so valiantly with his captors because he hoped to die at their hands. Sousa, he told the British envoy, was 'neither out of his wits, nor drunk, but the most insolent of all men living and calm as fanatics usually are'.

While the prisoner was brought in chains to Lisbon and tortured in the presence of Pombal and two judges, José stopped attending councils of state. A detachment of cavalry accompanied him on hunting expeditions and soldiers escorted him wherever he left the palace. 'He does not walk five yards from his coach but through the lines of his guards,' wrote the envoy on 13 January, 'and when he goes on Saturdays to hear mass in a convent in Lisbon, the guards are drawn up from the coach to the high altar.' For several months, the king was absent from all public audiences and, when he did reappear, he sat on a particularly high throne behind a balustrade.

José was aware of his own lack of education. No doubt encouraged by Pombal, he now gave orders that his elder grandson should receive more appropriate schooling. A few months earlier, Pombal had appointed Manuel do Cenáculo Vilas Boas, one of his most intelligent advisers, to be Prince José's confessor. Now Cenáculo (appointed Bishop of Beja) also took on the role of the prince's preceptor. He ensured the boy was taught history, geography, geometry and law, he provided books for him to read – including works by Erasmus and Racine – and he instilled in his mind a more secular approach to state affairs.

The new papal nuncio arrived in Lisbon on 28 May 1770, received with rapture by the people of the city who knelt on the river banks in their thousands as he was rowed across the Tagus to the Praça do Comércio. The *Te Deum* was sung in the royal chapel and, on 4 July, Maria engaged him in conversation when he came to Ajuda for his first official audience.

On 17 December, the nuncio gave a banquet to celebrate Maria's thirty-sixth birthday. It was a diplomatic gesture, given unusual significance because of the failure of the previous nuncio to celebrate her marriage ten years before. It should have been a happy occasion for Maria, blending her religious faith with the return of a papal nuncio and her happy conjugal life. Instead, it was tinged with anxiety, for her sister Doroteia lay dying in the *Barraca Real*.

Doroteia's mental health had deteriorated since she sang so sweetly in the concerts at Queluz. She had been ill for more than seven years, her condition described as 'hysteric, accompanied by an almost total lack of appetite which has reduced her to a state of extreme weakness'. The doctors prescribed constant bleedings, which weakened her further, and she died on 14 January 1771. She was thirty-one years old.

According to custom, the family confined themselves to the palace for eight days, after which they travelled to Salvaterra. Doroteia had not left the *Barraca Real* for several years; her death did not put a stop to the chase. Maria hunted deer and wild boar, and soon after her return to Ajuda in April, she conceived her sixth child. In the summer, she enjoyed the entertainments at Queluz and, on 22 September, she 'miscarried of a prince'.

Pombal was now at the zenith of his power. 'Age,' wrote an Englishmen who met him at this time, 'appeared neither to have diminished the vigour, freshness, nor activity of his faculties. In his person, he was very tall and slender; his face long, pale, meagre and full of intelligence.'[34]

Although he tolerated the return of the nuncio, Pombal continued his battle with the church. He had banished the Jesuits from the country and its colonies but he remained obsessed by them, attributing all events which angered him to a Jesuit conspiracy. France and Spain had followed his example and banished the order from their territories, and all three countries were now working through diplomatic channels to persuade the Pope to take more drastic action against the Society of Jesus

At the same time, Pombal was reforming the system of education which, until their expulsion from the country, had been run by Jesuits. He founded a College of Nobles with an enlightened curriculum (foreign languages, mathematics and the sciences); he opened a commercial college to teach book-keeping and commerce; and in 1772, he reformed the University of Coimbra. He established faculties of mathematics and science. He introduced Newtonian physics and ordered the construction of laboratories, a museum of natural history, and an observatory. He updated the faculty of medicine, allowing the dissection of corpses (which had previously been banned on religious grounds) and the study of hygiene ('because it is easier to conserve health than to recuperate it once lost').[35]

Pombal instigated these reforms in person in September 1772, the only time during his years as a minister that he travelled independently of the court. He made the journey to Coimbra in almost royal state, returning to Lisbon in late October to continue his machinations against the Jesuits. And ten months later, he achieved his ambition, receiving news from Rome which gave him 'the greatest satisfaction'. The Pope had succumbed to the pressure; he had abolished the Society of Jesus.

The papal bull was signed on 21 July 1773 and, according to Robert Walpole (the new British envoy), Pombal was 'highly gratified in this last step to the extinction of a body with which he has been contesting for so many years, especially as he must be allowed the merit of being the first in this country who ventured openly to attack the society'. In celebration, the *Te Deum* was sung in the churches, and the illuminations and rejoicings – which Pombal had ordered and which no-one dared disobey – lasted for three days.

7

The Succession

The king is very much out of humour.
Robert Walpole, 8 August 1774

The following January, a drama was played out in Salvaterra and Lisbon. It began as soon as the royal family arrived at the hunting lodge when, in a private conversation with one of the secretaries of state, Maria's mother was informed that there were plans afoot to change the succession.

Pombal was aware that his efforts to create a secular state would be reversed if Maria came to the throne. Her son, Prince José, had been educated by Cenáculo Vilas Boas for almost four years now. He was proving to be a studious pupil, absorbing his teacher's liberal opinions, and Pombal's intention was to bypass Maria's right to the throne and appoint her elder son as heir apparent (effectively introducing a Salic law). He had been working on this plan in great secret and only three people had any knowledge of it: Pombal, the king, and another secretary of state, José de Seabra e Silva.

José de Seabra ('a man of talents, great application and extensive knowledge') had endeared himself to Pombal in 1767 when he edited a book of anti-Jesuit propaganda, a book in which every ill in recent Portuguese history was laid firmly at the door of the Society of Jesus. Four years later, he was appointed secretary of state and soon became Pombal's unofficial second-in-command. He was in Pombal's confidence and it was generally assumed that he would, in time, take over the role of first minister. Seabra was on good terms with Mariana – and with Maria and Pedro – and he was unhappy about the plan to change the succession.

Pombal had not travelled with José to his country palaces for several years, preferring to remain in Lisbon to deal with matters of government. Other ministers followed the court and, in early January 1774, Seabra accompanied the royal family to Salvaterra where Pombal's absence gave him an opportunity to speak to the queen in confidence.

Mariana was a woman of spirit and ability, 'with a sound understanding and a cultivated mind'.[36] She never tried to gain power or achieve political influence, but she was suspicious of Pombal and this latest intrigue was too important to ignore. She told her daughter of the plot and Maria (now four months pregnant with her seventh child) stood up for herself, one of the few times she had the courage to do so.

She remembered the time she had almost died from a fever and *Senhor dos Passos* was brought to her bedroom. She remained convinced that the statue had saved her life. She also believed that God had preserved her life so she could inherit the throne and re-establish the power of the church. She was aware of her son's liberal education and feared that – if he came to the throne in her stead – he would endorse Pombal's secular policies.

So she went to see her father. Confident that she was acting in the interests of divine providence, she begged him to reconsider. Speaking with 'unusual energy and conviction', she told him that she would refuse to sign any paper renouncing her God-given right to the throne.[37] José soothed her and, now the secret was out, he realised that life in the palace would be impossible if he allowed Pombal to continue with his plan.

On 15 January, when he returned to Lisbon to attend the Devotion of Santa Engracia, José informed Pombal that there was a traitor in his service. He did not name the man or the nature of the treason, but since he had changed his mind about the succession, Pombal realised that it could only have been Seabra.

As Walpole put it, 'the Marquis de Pombal expects a great deal from those he has favoured and is of an unforgiving temper when his views are opposed'. He wrote a decree dismissing Seabra from his offices of state, exiling him to his father's estates in the country, and giving him twenty-four hours to leave the city. The king signed the decree on 16 January and, when Seabra arrived at Belém for the return journey to Salvaterra, he was ordered to go immediately to Pombal's house.

Seabra left Lisbon early next morning. In April, he was arrested and imprisoned in a fort near Oporto. 'The poor gentleman's fate,' wrote Walpole, 'is growing every day worse and worse.' In October, he sailed for Rio de Janeiro where he was held prisoner on an island until he was put on board another ship for Angola. He arrived in Luanda in March 1775 and was incarcerated in a fort at Pedras Negras, 'where he would have fallen victim to the climate had not an old Negro woman taken care of him'.[38]

This dramatic episode had severe repercussions for the royal family as well as for José de Seabra. The minister had been a favourite with Mariana and her daughter, and it is easy to imagine their shock when they learnt of his fate. It is also easy to imagine the family arguments that ensued. A few days later, Mariana fell ill, supposedly with rheumatism, and remained 'indisposed' for several months. At the same time, José stopped hunting – indeed, he stopped taking any exercise at all. He was 'a fat, bulky man' and, four weeks after Maria gave birth to a daughter (Clementina) on 9 June, he had his first stroke, suffering from 'a giddiness in the head' and weakness on one side of his body. As Walpole explained:

> This alteration in his state of health may have been brought upon him by a quick transition from a very active life to the more sedentary one which His Majesty has given himself up to since the beginning of the queen's illness at Salvaterra. Previous to this, he used to be out shooting six or eight hours every day, in all weathers and in all seasons, in the middle of the day even at the hottest time of the year.
>
> The king is of a sanguine complexion and has been very careless as to what he eats at his meals, which have been in

> general of the most savoury and unwholesome kind. He has for a number of years had swelled legs which are certain marks of a bad habit of body. These circumstances, added to that of His Majesty being arrived at an age which has been fatal to his family, makes his present state of health the more critical.

José never recovered his spirits. He was 'blooded frequently' and ordered to take the baths at Alcaçarias near Lisbon, but he remained 'in a dejected state and very much out of humour'. He refused to take exercise and an ulcer broke out on one of his legs. Mariana, too, remained weak. To Maria's dismay, her parents had lost their interest in life. They did not go into the country as usual in November, although they did (against doctors' advice) travel to Salvaterra in January where José suffered a number of strokes over the next few months.

They returned to Ajuda on 8 May. Four weeks later, on José's sixty-first birthday, a bronze statue of the king was inaugurated in the Praça do Comércio. Standing in the centre of the great square on the riverside, it depicted José on horseback, wearing a breast-plate and plumed helmet, his horse trampling on writhing serpents, the pedestal decorated with allegorical figures and a bas-relief of the Marquis de Pombal. Made from thirty tons of bronze, the statue was 'larger than any modern work of the kind and is cast entire'.

The Praça do Comércio was the centrepiece of Pombal's reconstruction of the city, although one side remained unfinished and this was hung with a painted replica. On 6 June 1775, the square was swept and sanded, the stands filled with members of the court, secretaries of state and foreign ministers, magistrates and city dignitaries. At three o'clock in the afternoon, after the royal family had taken their seats under a canopy, Pombal stepped forward to unveil the statue from its shroud of crimson silk. It was a ceremony of great pomp but José was tired after the journey from Salvaterra. The strokes had left him partially paralysed; he was unable to 'resist fatigue and the heat of the sun as he used to do'. He showed no signs of pleasure when the statue was unveiled.

A few days later, Pombal presented José with a report on his achievements as first minister of the country. It was a masterpiece of self-congratulation:

> Observant foreigners do not fail to remark the many millions that in a few years were spent on public and private buildings after the earthquake. They saw a most magnificent square, surpassing all others in Europe in size and beauty. They saw a costly and unexampled equestrian statue erected in that square ... They saw the streets rendered impassable by the multitude of sumptuous carriages. Every foreigner, I say, who observed such a reunion of riches could not but be convinced that the capital and kingdom were in the highest state of prosperity and opulence.[39]

The doctors now advised José to take the baths at Estoril, twelve miles west of Lisbon, and Pombal offered the use of his mansion house in Oeiras (midway between Lisbon and Estoril). The family made the journey on 3 July and stayed in Oeiras for three months. The house was grandiose and comfortable, surrounded by extensive grounds with citrus groves and vineyards, water cascades and a lake where Maria tried her hand at fishing.

José received some benefit from the waters at Estoril, although he continued to suffer from 'weakness of the limbs and a lowness of spirits'. His leg flared up again in early September and he confined himself to his bedchamber, 'very much dejected'. On the 20th, Walpole reported that 'the disorder in the king's leg is of a serious nature. He has been in great pain, relieved by a slight operation. He cannot move without help and continues very much dejected.'

The family returned to the *Barraca Real* in early October, a few days before a brutal public execution. Shortly before the inauguration of the king's statue, an elementary bomb was found in the house of João Baptiste Pele (an Italian living in Lisbon), together with a fifteen-hour fuse and two wax models of the key to Pombal's coach-house. It was assumed that Pele planned to place the bomb under the seat of Pombal's carriage the night before the ceremony. Convicted of high treason, his death on 11 October was cruel – even by the standards of the Inquisition. Having already been tortured on the rack, his hands were sliced off, his abdomen opened up and drawn. He was finally dismembered while still alive, pulled apart by four horses.

The morning after this gruesome execution, the royal family attended a *Te Deum* in celebration of Pombal's escape from death and José began to feel better. He ordered an opera to be performed in the *Barraca Real* and he went out shooting ('with some success'). In January 1776, the family moved to Salvaterra where José's leg deteriorated again and he remained in bed for several weeks. They returned to Ajuda at the end of May. And when Maria's two-year-old daughter Clementina died on 27 June, the king directed that there should be 'no court mourning for a princess of such tender years'.

By the end of July, José was back in bed with several ulcers on his leg and an intermittent fever. In October, he returned to the baths at Alcaçarias, immersing himself in the water for several hours a day. On 2 November, 'finding himself somewhat out of order', he remained in the palace. His wife was 'blooded by way of precaution'.

Four days later, he suffered another, more devastating stroke which affected the entire left side of his body. He lost the power of speech. He tried to speak but only made inarticulate sounds. Pombal attended the palace every day, his tall frame bending over the sickbed, but the ranks of courtiers closed around the king as soon as he left the room and foreign diplomats wrote home to their governments that a change in politics was imminent.

On 22 November, after 'copious bleedings and blisters', José asked to be given the last rites. And while prayers were read in the churches, he became fearful for his immortal soul. On 29 November, he banned Pombal from entering his rooms and appointed his 'very much beloved and esteemed wife' to act as regent on his behalf.

Pombal was seventy-eight years old. He stooped slightly, but his great height was still impressive and age had not impaired his vigour or his intellectual power. A few months earlier, the French ambassador had written that the minister was 'sound in body and mind, thinking himself immortal, talking of vast projects that not even his sons could hope to see realised'.[40] But he was loathed by the people, from the humblest citizen to members of the royal family; now even the king had turned against him.

While her mother took charge of affairs of state, Maria prepared herself for absolute power. Up to this moment, she had been allowed no control over her life, no influence over the pattern of her days. Soon she would have total control, not only over her own life, but over the lives of all her subjects. It was an awesome responsibility for a woman of her education and temperament. She was forty-three years old and the burden was harder to bear because she was about to give birth to her sixth (and final) child.

The baby was born prematurely on 22 December. It was a difficult birth and, for several days, Maria was 'very much indisposed'. She was declared out of danger by the end of the year but her newborn daughter was too weak to survive. The baby died on 14 January, José's health continued to deteriorate, and Walpole, writing discreetly about the shifting sands of power, 'was not idle in observing the motions of the different persons about the court'.

On 23 January, Pombal exerted his authority for the last time. There had been a disturbance in the fishing village of Trafaria, on the southern shore of the Tagus. Some of the villagers had roughed up an official. On the excuse that the village was a hotbed of deserters and vagrants, Pombal sent in the police with orders to set fire to the village. That night, the glow of burning houses stained the sky, the flames visible from the *Barraca Real* where José's family had gathered at his bedside.

The king was now 'taken out of bed for a few days' but the ulcers on his leg began to weep and fester, and like his father before him, he became bloated with oedema. Priests and friars gathered in his bedroom and, during his last days of life, he made two decisions. The first, written on a paper which he gave to his wife on 20 February, expressed his 'great desire' that his grandson (Prince José) should be married without delay to his youngest daughter (Benedita).

According to Robert Walpole, this marriage between aunt and nephew 'had long been determined upon and it cannot be doubted that Pombal was privy to it'. Papal dispensation had been obtained as early as October 1775, when the royal family was staying in Pombal's house in Oeiras, but the ceremony was delayed, partly because the bridegroom had not yet reached puberty and partly because the king hoped that his health would improve. He wanted the marriage to be a state occasion; he wanted to play his part with due pomp and magnificence. Now, at the very end of his life, he decided to go ahead with a marriage which he believed would ensure the succession of the Bragança dynasty.

The ceremony took place in the palace chapel during the afternoon of 21 February. Only the immediate family were present and, when it was over, they made their way to José's bedroom, knelt to kiss his hand, 'and retired very much affected'. The newly-married prince was fifteen years old, his body still changing from boy to man; his bride was thirty, full-bosomed and stout. There was little sexual attraction between them but that night, according to custom, Maria helped to undress her sister and prepare her for the marriage bed.

José's second decision was communicated to Maria in a personal letter. It began with the usual platitudes, that she should rule the country well, that she should look after her mother and sisters, that she should pay his debts and be kind to his servants. Finally, in the last words of a dying man, he asked her to 'remit the legal punishment of those state criminals she shall judge worthy of pardon. As to the crimes and offences which they have committed against my person or against the state, I have already pardoned them all, that God may pardon me my sins.'

Maria and her mother wasted no time. On 23 February, they revoked the imprisonments which had most distressed them. The Bishop of Coimbra was released from his dungeon near Lisbon and received that afternoon in the *Barraca Real*; Maria's disgraced uncles, bastard sons of João V, were ordered to return to the city, 'restored to the establishments they previously enjoyed'; and a letter was sent to recall José de Seabra from Angola.

The king died shortly after midnight on 24 February, 'finishing his life with such ease that it required the application of a mirror to determine his death with certainty'. Maria had retired from her father's room to rest but, when told of the news, 'she prepared to receive the ministers of state and admitted them into her presence to kiss her hand as sovereign'.

The following day, Pombal returned to the palace to be greeted with the words, 'Your Excellency has nothing more to do here'. Barred from royal circles, he returned home and hid behind the shuttered windows of his house while the people of Lisbon took to the streets, rejoicing. Maria ascended the throne on a wave of public enthusiasm. The first female monarch in Portuguese history, her accession was seen as a gift from God. The tyrant had fallen. The rule of the Marquis de Pombal was over.

Part Two

Absolute Power

8

Regime Change

... A dawn of brightest ray
Has boldly promised the returning day.
Beneath the smiles of a benignant queen
Boasts the fair opening of a reign serene
Of omen high ...
William Julius Mickle, 1779

According to custom, Maria and her family confined themselves to the palace for eight days. On 26 February, 'with the usual pomp and ceremony', the king's body was taken to the church of São Vicente de Fora. The following morning, Maria gave orders that the prisons be opened and more than eight hundred people – aristocrats, priests and magistrates, men, women and children – were released from the dungeons. They emerged pale and emaciated, their clothes in tatters, their eyes screwed up against the light. It was, wrote the Austrian ambassador, 'an image of the rising from the dead'.

Among them were forty-five Jesuits, including Timoteo de Oliveira, 'Her Majesty's former confessor whom she has always greatly missed'. Five aristocrats (the Marquis de Alorna, the Count de São Lourenço, and three brothers of the old Marquis de Távora) refused to accept their liberty until their innocence was confirmed by a tribunal, so Maria agreed to a temporary exile sixty miles from court.

Her most urgent problem was Pombal. He had written a letter of resignation ('on account of advanced age') to her mother on 5 February, a letter which Mariana ignored. He wrote again on 1 March, this time to Maria, begging for permission to retire to his estates in the country. Maria asked her mother for advice. 'I suppose he must be dismissed,' she is reported as saying, 'since everybody thinks he should be.'

Mariana knew well that Pombal had a powerful personality; he might even convince Maria that no-one else was capable of running the country, that there should at least be a hand-over to a new administration. 'In that case,' she told her daughter, 'avoid seeing him, even once, upon business.'[1]

So Maria accepted his resignation and, on 4 March, she signed a decree allowing him to retire to a town near his birthplace and ordering him to remain there. The decree was taken to Pombal's house and read aloud to him at two o'clock that afternoon, at which point – according to Walpole – the minister 'lost all his fortitude'. He set out immediately for his house in Oeiras and, that night, the people of Lisbon burned him in effigy and marched singing through the streets.

On the same day, Maria began to appoint a new cabinet. 'The clergy seem to be in great expectation of a return to their power under the new reign,' wrote Walpole on 26 February, 'and the nobility flatter themselves that they shall be restored to their former consideration and consequence.' Everyone had expectations of Maria and it must have been difficult for a woman with so little knowledge of public affairs to choose men to run the country.

It was important to have some continuity in state affairs so, on her mother's advice, she appointed two ministers who had served under Pombal: Aires de Sá e Melo as secretary of state for foreign affairs and Martinho de Melo e Castro as minister of marine and the colonies. Ten days later, she appointed two further secretaries of state: the Marquis de Angeja as president of the treasury (and first minister) and the Viscount de Ponte de Lima as secretary of state for home affairs. These men were new to government and both had reason to dislike the previous regime. Angeja's brother (Count de São Lourenço) and Ponte de Lima's father (Viscount de Vila Nova da Cerveira) had both been imprisoned by Pombal. Vila Nova had died in the dungeons.

Meanwhile, Pombal and his wife had left Oeiras on 7 March, heading north to their place of exile. They made slow progress. The roads were a quagmire from the winter rains and, to avoid angry villagers, they made several detours which prolonged the journey. Pombal was too depressed to leave the carriage but sometimes, to lighten the load on the mules, his wife was forced to walk. The party stumbled along, manoeuvring the carriage over the rough roads. At night they kept moving by the light of torches.

They arrived at their destination on 15 March. Pombal owned large estates in the area but had neglected to maintain his property in the town, so the only accommodation available was a small single-storey house in the market square. The walls were damp from the rain and there was little furniture, but they settled in as best they could and unpacked the few possessions they had been able to carry with them.

It had been – to put it mildly – a stressful few months. And Maria had hardly come to terms with her new position when she and her family fell ill with measles (only her husband and second son avoided the infection). Maria's symptoms began on 23 March and it was not until 27 April that she was well enough to meet with her ministers.

At the meeting, it was agreed that her acclamation would take place on 13 May in the Praça do Comércio. It was also confirmed that (under the Laws of Lamego) Pedro would have the status of king-consort with the title of Pedro III, but he would at all times be subordinate to his wife. He would walk on her left side, he would sign his name below hers, and he was not entitled to the crown. In the double portrait painted at about this time, Maria is depicted with her hand on the crown; Pedro's hand is hovering above it.

The morning of 13 May dawned bright and sunny. A pavilion had been erected in the Praça do Comércio with a gallery of twenty-eight arches supported by marbled columns. Decorated with military emblems and allegorical figures, it was 'magnificently furnished with tapestries and damasks and adorned with gold fringes and lace'. Crowds had gathered during the night, singing and dancing through the early hours of the morning, and now the square was packed with people, the river crowded with boats filled with spectators. People were crammed onto every balcony and rooftop, with a few brave souls perched at perilous height on José's equestrian statue in the centre of the square.

The royal family arrived in the afternoon and, at four o'clock, the procession formed and began to move into the gallery. First came the heralds and knights-at-arms, followed by the aristocrats, the religious establishment, and the secretaries of state. Then came Maria's two sons, Crown Prince José (now known as the Prince of Brazil) and Prince João, followed by Pedro with his entourage. Maria's consort wore a cloak of flame-coloured stripes, his robes studded with diamonds. Over a long bag-wig, he wore a hat adorned with white feathers and he carried a sword of solid gold.

Finally Maria appeared, followed by the ladies of her household. She looked magnificent. She wore a robe of silk taffeta woven with silver thread and covered with diamonds, the bodice encrusted with precious stones set in a floral design. Her train was made from cloth of gold and she wore the mantle of state, a crimson cloak embroidered with gold and silver thread.

The royal musicians played as the procession entered the gallery and the family took their seats under a silk canopy. After several declarations were read in ringing tones, Maria knelt on a crimson cushion and, in a quiet voice, promised to govern her country well, administer justice, and guard the customs, privileges and liberties of her people. Her husband and sons paid her homage, her courtiers swore allegiance, and the royal standard-bearer acclaimed her as queen. Trumpets and bugles sounded, the crowds shouted '*Viva Rainha*', bells pealed, guns thundered a salute, rockets were launched into the sky. It was an amazing cacophony of sound; never, it seemed, had a monarch been acclaimed with such enthusiasm.

Maria herself looked solemn throughout the proceedings; according to a spectator, she appeared 'painfully affected and seemed to take no share in the general joy'.[2] Tired from the events of the last few months, still weak from the measles, she had been warned of a plot to incite the crowd into demanding the head of Pombal. Soldiers had surrounded the area, troops on horseback were ready to move at the first sign of unrest, but she was still unnerved by the occasional shout of 'Death to Pombal!' which rang out from the mass of people in the square.

When the ceremony was over, as she was leaving the gallery with the sceptre in her hand, the crowd broke through the barriers. The people knelt at her feet, they kissed the hem of her dress and train. There was such a throng around her that she was prevented from reaching the carriage waiting to take her home to the *Barraca Real*. Touched by this demonstration of affection, she told the guards not to intervene. She stood there for several minutes, surrounded by her subjects, 'affected almost to tears'.[3]

Four days later, Maria confirmed the innocence of the five noblemen who had refused to accept their liberty. On 22 May, Corpus Christi, she sat in a richly-decorated pavilion near the cathedral and watched her husband and sons walk in procession through the city. On 6 June, she took part in a new festival which she had dedicated to the Heart of Jesus. The following day, she moved to Queluz.

The palace had been unoccupied since her father suffered his first stroke in July 1774. Now, three years later, the servants opened the doors and windows, furniture and furnishings were brought from the *Barraca Real*, and the royal family drove out of Lisbon in a train of carriages and two-wheeled chaises. It was the hottest summer for almost thirty years and Maria took refuge in the formal gardens, shaded by trees imported from northern Europe, cooled by the fountains and running water. She stayed at Queluz for four months, enjoying excursions into the countryside and spending time in the Moorish palace at Sintra.

The only shadow on this summer idyll was her husband's health. On the morning of 16 August, Pedro suffered a minor stroke, 'taken ill while at mass with a giddiness in his head and he lay speechless for some time'. He remained unwell for several weeks but, after 'bleedings and other remedies', he recovered by the end of September. The family returned to Ajuda on 11 October and, ten days later, they set out on a three-day journey to the palace of Vila Viçosa.

One of the most pressing matters of state when José died was the situation in South America, where Portugal and Spain had been embroiled in territorial disputes for several years. Pombal had taken a particularly hard line on the matter and, by July 1776, it was feared that war would break out between the two countries. Maria was horrified by the prospect but, when she announced that she would give up the throne rather than go to war, her mother advised her to speak with more caution. As Robert Walpole put it, 'the queen mother, who has a spirit of more fortitude than the reigning queen, is not less solicitous of seconding her daughter's pacific views but says that this must be done with decency to the crown of Portugal'.

It was Mariana who made the first moves, exchanging letters of peace with her brother, Charles III of Spain. Formal negotiations began in May 1777 and, on 21 June, Walpole reported a 'suspension of hostilities' in the South American colonies. By August, Mariana and her brother were 'writing to each other every fortnight' and, in October, the two countries signed a treaty 'setting the limits of territory in South America'. This put an end to the territorial squabbles and formed the basis of a second treaty – of 'friendship and protection' – which was signed six months later.

Mariana undertook many of these negotiations personally and it was soon agreed that she should visit her brother in Spain. Her family travelled with her to the border, leaving Lisbon for Vila Viçosa on 21 October. Seven days later, Maria accompanied her mother to the river Caya (which formed the frontier between the border towns of Elvas and Badajoz) and there they took leave of each other 'with much tenderness on both sides'.

During the next four months, Mariana continued to negotiate the second treaty which was signed in March 1778. This was good timing, for Britain's War of Independence with its American colonies soon became a wider conflict. France entered the war in early 1778, followed by Spain a year later, so the treaty with Spain allowed Maria (despite the Anglo-Portuguese alliance and pressure from Britain to honour her obligations) to maintain a policy of 'the most strict neutrality'.

Mariana stayed in the Spanish court for a year and, to strengthen the links between the two countries, she discussed the betrothals of two of Maria's children to members of her brother's family. In June 1778, she was once more 'seized with the rheumatism' and was confined to bed for several weeks in the palace at Aranjuez. In July, she took the waters for eighteen days and, by mid-August, she was well enough to be 'pushed about the gardens in an old-fashioned cariole or three-wheeled chair'.[4]

When she returned to Portugal in November, Maria and Pedro travelled to Vila Viçosa to meet her. As her carriage descended into the valley from Badajoz, crowds of people lined the roads on both sides of the frontier to watch the royal reunion on the banks of the river Caya. Next day, a hunt was scheduled at Vila Viçosa. Mariana was now suffering from heart disease as well as arthritis; she could no longer ride on horseback but nothing could deter her from the chase. Following the hunt in a sedan chair, she shot three stags and thirteen deer.

The family left Vila Viçosa on 10 December, arriving in Lisbon three days later. On the 17th, Maria celebrated her forty-fourth birthday with a *beija-mão* in Ajuda, followed by the opening performance in the new theatre at Queluz, an opera composed by her music teacher, David Perez.

9

The Shadow of Pombal

The Marquis de Pombal is a criminal worthy of exemplary punishment.
Maria I, 16 August 1781

While her mother negotiated treaties with Spain and laid the foundations for two dynastic marriages, Maria set about restoring the power of the church. She dismissed Cenáculo Vilas Boas, her son's liberal-minded preceptor, and wrote a public letter to Miguel da Anunciação, reinstating him as Bishop of Coimbra and referring to 'the great confidence and esteem which I have for you'. She had no power to revive the Society of Jesus but she did her best to make amends for Pombal's persecution of the order. She gave pensions to Jesuits released from jail, sent money to the Pope to cover the cost of supporting priests in exile, and restored the names of Jesuit saints to the calendar of religious festivals.

She re-established the jurisdiction of the papal nuncio's court and admonished members of the clergy who had embraced Pombal's more liberal ideas. She rewarded people of other faiths who converted to Catholicism and stood godmother at their baptisms. And she fulfilled the vow made on her wedding night, to build a church and convent dedicated to the Heart of Jesus if she was blessed with the birth of a son. She selected a site in Estrela, a suburb to the west of Lisbon, and appointed an architect to design an immense building in late baroque and neo-classical style.

Meanwhile, her ministers had inherited a chaotic situation. The state papers of the previous reign were stored in great disorder in Pombal's house in Lisbon, so two officials were appointed to organise a filing system. The treasury was so depleted that Angeja had to instigate an economy campaign. He suspended the works of reconstruction in the city, cut expenditure on the royal opera, reorganised the system of palace servants, and reduced the number of horses and mules in the royal stables. It was said that these measures produced significant savings, but because Maria was giving so much to the church, they made little difference to treasury funds.

In all such matters, the secretaries of state could only advise their sovereign; it was Maria who made the decisions. Her ministers were dutiful and pious men, but only two of them had any experience of world affairs. They were restricted by the formality of the court, unable to make judgements on the queen's behalf. 'Her Majesty is above the law,' Ponte de Lima explained to Robert Walpole, 'no minister can tie her hand or circumscribe her authority.'

This was an impossible position for anyone of such limited education and experience, even more so for a woman who often yearned for the cloistered life of a nun. 'She is truly worthy of esteem and respect,' wrote a visitor to Portugal in the summer of 1777, 'but she has not the qualities that make a great queen. No-one can be kinder, more charitable, or more sensitive, but these good qualities are marred by an excessive and ill-judged religious devotion.'[5]

Walpole put it more succinctly. 'The queen is timid,' he wrote, 'easily influenced by the clergy and of unlimited obedience to the See of Rome and the jurisdiction of the clergy in its most extensive pretensions.' Her husband was no help in state affairs. According to Walpole, Pedro was 'of a confined understanding. He hears three or four masses in the morning in the utmost ecstasy and attends evening prayers as devoutly. He speaks much in precepts of goodness and justice but, as he has no knowledge of mankind or business, he is easily governed by those immediately about him, especially if they belong to the church.'

Maria did her best to rise to the occasion. She took her council of state seriously and tried to understand matters of government and discuss them with her ministers. She relied on her mother for advice in political matters and she also turned to Inácio de São Caetano, a jovial man of humble birth who had served as her confessor for twenty years and did not hesitate to involve himself in affairs of state.

At the same time, she took 'every means to announce a reign of clemency'. She gave pensions and court appointments to men released from prison or returning from exile. She restored the freedom of the press (which had been abolished by Pombal). She inaugurated a Royal Academy of Sciences and encouraged expeditions to record the flora and fauna of the colonies. And remembering the brutality of the Távora and Pele executions, she announced that she would not sanction the death penalty, 'even for the greatest criminals'.

Maria had exiled Pombal to a small town eighty miles north of Lisbon but members of the nobility – particularly those who had languished in dungeons – were calling for stronger punishment; some even lobbied for his execution. Maria understood their anger, but Pombal was José's favoured and trusted minister and she honoured her father's memory.

In early 1779, a returning exile made a claim for damages against Pombal, accusing him of 'having abused a despotic power to raise himself to the summit of honours and riches at the expense of the liberties of many innocent persons'.[6] Pombal responded with enthusiasm, drafting a closely-argued defence of his actions. It was the king, he wrote, who had signed every edict against the nobles and the Jesuits. He, the loyal servant, had merely been a passive instrument in his master's service.

When Maria heard of Pombal's defence, she asked for a copy and was deeply upset to find her father held publicly responsible for such tyranny. She discussed the matter with her mother and, on 3 September, she declared the defence to be libellous, an insult to her father's memory. She also gave in to the demands of her courtiers, ordering an official prosecution on charges of abuse of power, corruption and fraud.

Two judges made the journey to Pombal's house where they set up a temporary courtroom. Their interrogations began on 11 October and lasted for more than three months. Pombal's strength was fading. Sometimes he fainted, sometimes he was carried into the courtroom on a stretcher, sometimes he was too ill to be questioned. But throughout the trial, he continued to maintain that every cruel deed, every act of terror, had been instigated by José who had signed all the relevant papers.

In January 1780, the judges travelled to Salvaterra to report their findings to Maria. They had learnt nothing of significance; their report contained no grounds for further punishment. Pombal was now eighty years old and in failing health. Hoping the matter would soon be taken out of her hands, Maria sent a doctor to report on his condition. The old man's physical sufferings may have been acute but his brain was as sharp as ever. On 7 March, to Maria's dismay, the doctor reported that Pombal retained 'the vivacity of spirit, the lucidity and firmness of intellect, the fresh and exact memory of a man not thirty years old'.[7]

Two months later, the Marquis de Alorna (son-in-law of the old Marquis de Távora) called for the verdicts of January 1759 to be revoked. He and the surviving Távoras had been declared innocent in May 1777, it was known that the Duke de Aveiro had retracted his confession (which had been obtained on the rack) before his execution, and there were other irregularities at the time of the trial.

Maria believed in the innocence of the Távoras. She was also aware that a posthumous pardon would damage the honour of her father. It took courage to sign an edict which declared the verdicts to be 'null and unjust' and appointed a tribunal of magistrates to review the evidence. The edict was dated 9 October 1780 and, as soon as she had signed her name, she threw her pen on the floor and had a fit of hysterics. Screaming that she was damned, condemned to hell for all eternity, she had to be lifted bodily out of her chair and carried from the room.

This was Maria's first major breakdown, a torrent of conflicting emotions exacerbated by the ill-health of both her husband and her mother. Pedro had suffered a second stroke in July 1779, taken ill during a performance in the theatre at Queluz. One of his legs was affected and he found himself unable to speak. A few days later, after 'frequent bleedings and other treatments, his speech and mouth are somewhat restored to their former state but his leg is still impaired'.

The doctors recommended that he take the baths at Alcaçarias, but Pedro 'omitted taking them upon various pretences, being much averse to them, and the distance from Queluz being too great to undertake that remedy with safety'. It was therefore decided to convert the Senate House in the Praça do Comércio into royal apartments. Builders worked 'day and night with the greatest dispatch' to prepare the building and the family moved into their new accommodation at the end of August.

Mariana, meanwhile, was suffering from her old complaint ('much afflicted with the rheumatism'), as well as from pains in her chest. In September 1780, she travelled to Caldas to take the waters and, as the year drew to a close, she was 'attacked with a violent oppression at her breast which has given the greatest alarm'. She received the last rites from the papal nuncio and died in the *Barraca Real* on 15 January 1781. It was, Maria wrote to her uncle in Spain, 'such a painful blow for she was a precious companion in every way.'[8]

Maria had relied on her mother's support in all matters of government but on 23 May, when the tribunal of magistrates reported its findings, she had to deal with the situation alone. In a lengthy report which deplored the use of torture and discredited some of the evidence, the tribunal confirmed the innocence of the Távora family (but upheld the verdict on the Duke de Aveiro). Although this established the guilt of Pombal, it was a devastating report for Maria who perceived it as a reproach to her father who had signed the death warrants.

Three weeks later, her convent at Estrela was ready for occupation. Maria took a personal interest in the opening ceremonies and, on 16 June – 'with the greatest pomp' – the abbess and sixteen nuns arrived at the convent in a train of royal carriages.

Mass was celebrated in the presence of the royal family and the court, after which the nuns ate their first meal in the refectory, a meal prepared in the palace kitchens and served – to the nuns' amazement – by the queen's own hands.

This should have been one of the happiest moments of Maria's life, an occasion which combined her royal status with her inclinations towards convent life and her love for the Heart of Jesus, but the problem of Pombal lay heavily on her mind. Her confessor had taken on her mother's role of adviser and confidante, and on his recommendation, she finally made a decision. Her decree, dated 16 August, was remarkably charitable:

> The Marquis de Pombal is a criminal worthy of exemplary punishment, but out of regard for his advanced age and heavy infirmities, and consulting my clemency rather than my justice ... I remit all bodily punishments and enjoin him to absent himself from the court at a distance of at least twenty leagues, my intention being only to pardon him the personal chastisement which justice and the laws require.[9]

This went some way towards meeting the demands of her courtiers, although the decree made little difference to Pombal, whose place of exile was twenty-eight leagues from court and whose iron constitution was crumbling at last. His skin was ulcerated, his blood poisoned, and he was suffering from fever and dysentery. The doctors prescribed asses' milk and viper-broth (local people brought snakes to his door in baskets) and he was dosed with quinine.

Maria had allowed his two sons to retain their honours and position, and as Pombal's health deteriorated, she gave them permission to leave the court. 'Be good sons,' she told them, 'go and look after your father.'

10

The Double Marriage

Expect neither a fair wind nor a good marriage from Spain.
Portuguese proverb

Pombal died on 8 May 1782, lifting the shadow which had darkened Maria's life for more than quarter of a century. The next four years were the most relaxed and happy of her reign, although life at court remained stiff with formality. Nothing had changed since the days of her grandfather, João V, who had been a stickler for protocol. With the unique exception of Maria's confessor, no person was allowed to sit in her presence. Everyone else had to stand or kneel – even the secretaries of state who attended the queen on matters of government.

This had been a problem for Pombal who suffered from varicose veins and leg ulcers. In early 1768, the government came to a standstill when he sprained his ankle. He continued to work and travel in his carriage, but the injury took time to heal and he was prevented from meeting José on business for three months, 'being unable to stand and kneel which the etiquette of this court requires'.

From time to time, Maria's courtiers would retire from her presence to lie down on the floors of antechambers. When talking or playing cards, her gentlemen-in-waiting were permitted to drop to one knee; the ladies were sometimes allowed to sit cross-legged on the floor. Her favourite courtier, the Marquis de Marialva, admitted to William Beckford (a wealthy Englishman who had become his friend) that attending the royal family was a tedious and tiring servitude. Beckford put it more bluntly, calling it 'a state of downright slavery'.

Beckford arrived in Portugal after a homosexual affair with a young aristocrat resulted in social ostracism at home. He was also shunned by the English community in Lisbon. Robert Walpole refused to present him at court, so protocol prevented him from paying his respects to the queen. One summer evening, when the royal family arrived at Marialva's house for an entertainment, he hid behind a window to watch Maria and Benedita take their seats for tea. 'The Viscount de Ponte de Lima knelt by the royal personages with abject devotion,' he wrote in his diary that night, 'and when the lord-in-waiting handed the tea to the queen and princess, he fell down on both knees to present it.'

Meanwhile, Maria's two sons 'stalked about with their hands in their pockets, their mouths in a perpetual yawn, their eyes wandering from object to object with a stare of royal vacancy. Few princes are more to be pitied than these, condemned by a ridiculous etiquette to strict confinement, never allowed to mix with the crowd.'[10]

In December 1782, Prince João (now fifteen years old) fell ill with smallpox. He began to feel unwell on the 26th while the court was making plans for the journey to Salvaterra, complaining of pains in his head and back. A fever set in and red spots appeared on his skin. The spots turned into pimples and then into blisters containing a pale yellow liquid.

Smallpox was a common disease. The mortality rate was about one in five and victims who survived an attack were often scarred for life. A mild or benign attack involved only a few blisters; when the blisters joined up all over the body, it was known as a confluent attack and was often fatal.

Initially, the doctors feared the worst, João's blisters 'having the appearance of the confluent sort'. By mid-January, they had changed their minds. The attack was benign, they said, so Maria left for Salvaterra on the 18th, leaving her son to convalesce in the *Barraca Real*. 'He gave me quite a fright as his load of pox blisters was very heavy,' she wrote to a cousin in Spain, 'but he has already left his bed and all he has to do now is to convalesce.'[11] She enjoyed the hunting at Salvaterra and, when João arrived on 15 February, she was delighted to find him 'fully recovered and not much changed in his appearance'.[12]

By this time, Pedro was suffering from an ulcer on one of his legs. This prevented him from riding on horseback and it continued to trouble him on his return to Ajuda. As Maria wrote on 6 April, 'the ailment, although it causes no alarm, mortifies him so we cannot enjoy the good weather'.[13] The ulcer had improved by July when they moved to Queluz; Pedro still had 'the remains of a sore' but he was well enough to accompany his family on excursions into the countryside.

On 10 August, they set out on a more unusual outing, a visit to the mansion house in Oeiras, now owned by Pombal's elder son. According to Pedro, they made the journey to inspect the formal gardens and the water cascades, but Maria also made the visit as a kindness to Pombal's family. Arriving in the mid-afternoon, they were taken around the gardens, strolling through the alleys of orange and lemon trees, visiting the waterfalls and stopping at the lake where – once again – Maria tried her hand at fishing. In the evening, a *merenda* was served in the house and as the family climbed into their chaises for the return journey to Queluz, two candles were placed in every window to illuminate the darkness.

A few days later, they moved to the convent-palace at Mafra where, on 2 September, Pedro suffered his third stroke. 'Being on a walk in the open air,' wrote the British consul (standing in for Walpole who was on leave in England), 'he was seized with a paralytic affliction in his mouth, from which he recovered sufficiently to resume his exercise, but three days later, he had a return of an old infection in one of his legs.'

The ulcer kept him in bed for ten days, so the family delayed their return to Queluz until the end of the month. In October, he made several public appearances, 'yet reports from within the palace are not uniformly favourable'. Pedro was sixty-six years old, older than both his father and brother when they died from the same condition. The strokes should have been taken as a warning but, on 24 November, Maria felt able to write that her husband's health was 'entirely better'.[14]

Pedro remained well through the winter and spring, and on 13 May 1784, there were great celebrations for Prince João's seventeenth birthday. A few days later, the family set out to enjoy the annual festival of Nossa Senhora do Cabo. They boarded ship at Belém and sailed down the coast to the Setúbal peninsula where campaign tents had been set up for their accommodation. For three days, they enjoyed bullfights, horsemanship displays, and grand processions; at night, there were concerts and fireworks.

This was the last time that Maria's three children would celebrate a spring festival together. The marriage negotiations with Spain had been finalised a few months earlier. Maria's daughter, Mariana, was pledged to Gabriel de Bourbon, fourth and favourite son of Charles III; her second son, João, was pledged to the eight-year-old Carlota Joaquina, daughter of Charles's eldest son. Arrangements for the ceremonies were made during the next ten months and, as the date of the nuptials approached, special couriers travelled between the courts with last-minute adjustments of detail.

It was customary in royal marriages for the ambassador of the bridegroom's country to make a formal demand for the bride. The Spanish and Portuguese ambassadors were to make their demands in Lisbon and Madrid on 27 March 1785, the marriages to be celebrated by proxy the following day, but Prince João fell ill with measles a few days before the demand for his sister, so the proceedings in Lisbon were delayed.

On 2 April, news arrived of the proxy marriage between João and Carlota in Spain (which had taken place on schedule), news celebrated with a *Te Deum* in the royal chapel. João was now feeling better and the demand for his sister took place during the afternoon of 11 April. The Spanish ambassador drove to the Praça do Comércio in a procession of seventy-five coaches accompanied by more than a hundred men on horseback. He was received by Maria and Pedro in the Senate House and, on behalf of Gabriel de Bourbon, made the formal demand for their daughter.

The marriage by proxy took place the following afternoon, an entire wedding ceremony 'conducted with all due pomp and magnificence' in the chapel of the *Barraca Real*. Maria gave her daughter away, Pedro stood proxy for Gabriel, and when the formalities were over, the Spanish ambassador made his way to Mariana's apartment and gave her a likeness of her husband. It was the first time she had seen his face.

That evening, there were fireworks and concerts and the whole of Lisbon was in gala. Walpole was amazed at the cost of it all:

> When I consider the very great quantity of clothes and laces and everything belonging to the toilet, of the finest and of the greatest magnificence, as well as several new carriages, and also the presents that are to be made to the same extent and in as great a number as those to be given by the king of Spain, I am entirely lost in the excess of expense that will accompany the completion of these marriages. Her Majesty has already given the Spanish ambassador her picture very richly set in diamonds, of a value very much beyond that of a usual present to an ambassador.

This was indeed a different approach from Maria's marriage twenty-five years earlier, when her father ensured that 'the nobility and gentry are put to no expense, not so much as the additional cost of a suit of clothes'.

The family set out for Vila Viçosa on 22 April, crossing the Tagus on royal barges, then travelling overland in 'five four-wheeled carriages accompanied by a numerous and splendid train of courtiers'. The first night of the journey was spent in Vendas Novas (the palace built by João V to house the court when it travelled to the frontier in 1729), the second night in the bishop's palace at Evora.

The Spanish princess left Aranjuez on 27 April, reaching Badajoz on 7 May. The following morning, her cortège descended into the valley, crossed the river Caya, and travelled on to Vila Viçosa. As her carriage arrived in the palace square, the guns of the castle and the regiments drawn up on parade gave her three twenty-one-gun salutes. Prince João helped her alight from the carriage; José and Benedita welcomed her to Portugal.

Maria and Pedro were waiting inside the palace and, as Carlota made her entrance, they were surprised and disturbed by what they saw. For Carlota was not only a child, she was extremely small for her age and unattractive in appearance, with frizzy hair and ungainly features. That evening, Maria wrote a disingenuous letter to her uncle in Madrid, informing him 'of the safe arrival of our beloved Carlota, who is so pretty and lively and grown-up for her age'.[15]

Carlota's retinue was to stay in Vila Viçosa for four days, after which it would accompany Maria's sixteen-year-old daughter across the border to Badajoz and on to Aranjuez to meet her husband. In the meantime, the court was in gala as Portuguese and Spanish nobility mixed for the first time in fifty-six years. Maria and her family (who normally ate alone in their separate apartments) dined together and in public to the sound of trumpets and kettle drums. In the evenings, the royal musicians played, Maria's sisters sang arias, and fireworks exploded into the sky.

Maria attended these celebrations with a heavy heart. She was about to lose her only daughter; it was unlikely they would meet again. She and Mariana said their farewells in private during the night of 11 May. The following morning, alone in her bedroom, Maria heard the twenty-one-gun salute, she heard Mariana's carriage rumble across the palace square. She knew the road the carriage would take. Eight years earlier, she had accompanied her mother to Elvas and down to the river Caya, but it would have been too distressing to make the same journey with her daughter, to perform their final embrace in public.

A few hours later, the family mounted their horses. João was as miserable as his mother and galloping after deer in the hunting park did little to take their minds off their loss. 'As soon as we reached the first thicket,' he wrote to his sister that night, 'there was a great storm which crowned this sad and bitter day, a day when I passed not a single moment without tears in my eyes.'[16]

Mariana arrived in Aranjuez on 23 May. The following morning, she wrote to her mother, a letter which described her husband and gave details of their first night together. Maria showed the letter to João and he wrote again to his sister:

> It is good what you said in your letter about your husband, that he likes you very much, that you feel the same way towards him, and that you are having very little sleep. I should like to take possession of my wife also. She is very small, but the time will come when I can do the same things to her as your husband does to you.[17]

1 Terreiro do Paço and the royal palace in Lisbon, 1693. João V built a new marble quay by the waterside but little else had changed by the time Maria was born here in 1734.

2 Palace of Queluz. Garden façade built by Pedro, completed in 1752.

3 Marquis de Pombal, painted after he was granted his title in 1769.

4 Maria I and her consort Pedro III, painted after her acclamation in 1777. Maria's hand is placed on the crown, signifying her role as monarch; Pedro's hand is hovering above it, signifying his more humble role as king-consort.

5 Maria I, c.1780. Engraving from original miniature portrait.

6 Prince José, aged 15, painted after his mother's acclamation in 1777.

7 Benedita, sister of Maria I and wife of Prince José, c.1785.

8 Carlota Joaquina, copy of a portrait painted in Spain shortly before her marriage to Prince João in 1785.

9 Prince João, c.1799. Engraving from original miniature portrait.

10 Maria I. Painting in original frame, copy of a portrait painted from life by the English artist, Thomas Hickey, in 1783.

11 Dr Francis Willis, painted after his 'cure' of George III in 1789.

12 William Stephens, owner of the royal glassworks at Marinha Grande.

13 Stephens's mansion house in Marinha Grande. Maria spent two nights here in 1788 and 'liked her situation so well that she regretted leaving'.

14 Dona Maria Pavilion at the palace of Queluz. Maria was kept hidden here for almost twelve years until the royal family fled to Brazil in November 1807.

15 Largo do Paço, Rio de Janeiro, as it was when Maria arrived here in March 1808. The royal palace (originally the viceroy's residence) is on the left. At right angles to the palace is the convent where Maria spent the last eight years of her life.

11

Bereavement

I miss him very much and have lost such good company.
Maria I, 6 June 1786

The family returned to Lisbon on 8 June. The following afternoon, João and Carlota were married in person in the chapel of the *Barraca Real*. And during the ceremony – a portent of things to come – the bride turned her head and bit her husband on the ear.

It was no longer believed that José and Benedita (now thirty-seven years old) would have children, so the marriage of Maria's second son was of paramount importance to the Bragança dynasty. The ceremony was followed by the usual three-day celebrations, during which the royal family attended a firework display in the Praça do Comércio, but the people of Lisbon showed no joy at the occasion. They were unimpressed by Carlota and made the comment that, in the exchange of princesses, they had given away a grown fish in exchange for a sardine.

João was also unhappy. He was ambivalent about his child bride and heartbroken at the loss of his sister, from whom he had been inseparable throughout childhood. He wrote to Mariana every week, letters which describe his grief at her absence. 'I miss you so much,' he wrote on 17 June after the family moved to Queluz. 'I cry every time I pass your bedroom door because it reminds me of our great conversations.'

Mariana, too, wrote every week and a letter which arrived towards the end of June gave Maria cause for concern. Her daughter had been married in person on 23 May and, as she learnt in Vila Viçosa, the marriage had been consummated with no difficulty. But the shock of the journey, finding herself alone in a foreign court, and going to bed with a man who was still a stranger, had affected Mariana's body which was responding to the strain by almost continual bleeding. 'I should like to know when you are expecting,' wrote João rather obliquely, 'because today I heard my mother mutter through clenched teeth that you had that thing again – well, you know what I mean.'[18]

Carlota, meanwhile, was proving to be vivacious, energetic and badly behaved. She refused to get up in the morning; she refused to get dressed, complaining about corsets and uncomfortable shoes; she ate with her hands at mealtimes and threw food at her husband; she remained mute during her lessons. João tried to act as an older brother; at first, he was even a little impressed. 'She is very clever and has lots of common sense for one who is still so little,' he wrote to his sister, but then added that his bride was 'very uninhibited, without any shame whatsoever'.[19]

Maria took on a motherly role and became the only person capable of keeping the unruly child in check. It was she who disciplined Carlota, threatening to withdraw her favourite activities – riding on donkey back or driving through the grounds of Queluz in a pony cart. She taught the child Portuguese phrases, they went riding together and visited convents, but it was hard work for Maria and the strain soon led to an attack of conjunctivitis.

Her eyes were still red and sore in mid-November when a special courier arrived from Spain. Mariana's body had settled down during the summer; she was expecting a child. Maria was delighted by the news but João was unsettled. Nineteen years old, too shy to seek an outlet elsewhere, he longed to get his hands on his little wife. 'It will be many years before I can go to her, which is mortifying,' he wrote to his sister. 'There can be no pleasure for now as she is so young and her body so small, but the time will come when I shall play with her. How happy I shall be then!'[20]

There was smallpox in Belém during the autumn of 1785. Prince José had never shown signs of the disease, so Maria delayed their return to the *Barraca Real* until 'the contagion had diminished' in early December. Three months later, Carlota suffered an infestation of head lice. 'You wouldn't believe the amount of lice she had,' João told his sister, 'they are like a plague.' Her scalp was wet with weeping sores so they shaved off her thick unruly hair, leaving only a forelock to grace the front of a cap. Confined to her apartments until her scalp dried out, she was visited twice a day by João who, 'playing donkey for her amusement', circled around the room on his hands and knees while his child-wife rode jockey-style on his back.[21]

Carlota's hair had grown to a halo of brown frizz when the family made plans to travel to Caldas da Rainha in early May. But Pedro felt unwell and the journey was postponed. During the next eight days, he suffered 'repeated paralytic attacks until he was seized on Saturday night, the 20th, with an apoplexy and, from that time, has remained in a situation beyond all hopes of recovery and without any symptoms of life, except the motion of the lungs and pulse, until Thursday morning when His Majesty expired'.

Pedro died early in the morning of 25 May. Later that day, Maria issued a statement. According to custom, 'and in demonstration of her grief', she would confine herself to the *Barraca Real* for eight days, after which the court would go into mourning for a year, 'six months deep and six months slight'. On the evening of 27 May, she kissed her husband's hand for the last time as the coffin left the palace on its way to the church of São Vicente de Fora.

Because of her advanced state of pregnancy, Mariana was not told of her father's illness, nor was she informed of his death until several weeks after she had given birth. 'I am very sorry for the cruel blow you are about to receive,' João wrote to his sister on 28 July, before giving her a detailed description of recent events. At first, Pedro had experienced 'a great tightness in his voice'. The doctors had applied leeches and Maria suggested that he remain in bed during João's birthday reception on 13 May ('which was very hard for him – you know what his temper was like'). The following day, Pedro insisted on leaving the palace:

> He was walking very slowly and when he came back, he took twenty-five minutes to reach his room. He sat down on his chair and stared at us in a daze and he would not speak unless we spoke to him. My mother asked him if he wanted to write to you. He said "yes" and then he wrote nonsense and we were all quite dismayed, and when he relieved himself, he did it in his chair. He could no longer stand.

Pedro was put to bed. Next morning, when he tried to get up:

> His legs were useless which scared us very much. Then he went to his chair and held himself up by his arms, still dazed and staring at us. All he would say was "yes" or "no". He was purged in the afternoon. It worked well but, after the last motion, we found him even weaker, so he was put to bed again.

On the morning of the 16th, the doctors applied blistering ointments, priests gave him the last rites ('which he received as best he could'), and Maria ordered that sacred images be brought to the palace. Four days later, Pedro 'began sweating and was soon soaked', after which more blistering ointment was applied, this time to his forehead. The priests anointed him and gave him absolution, 'and gradually he stopped taking anything other than little sips of breast milk'. On 24 May, João went to see his father just before midnight:

> He looked the same as he had on previous nights. He did not look as if he was dying. He was very florid and the veins all over his face were engorged. Then it struck twelve and, within a quarter of an hour, he started agonising until half past two in the morning when he died.

Maria was not in the room at the time. Pedro had remained in the same state for four days and she had no idea that he would die so suddenly. She had retired to bed in an adjoining room, tired out from worry and distress, and was sleeping soundly through the night. João waited until she woke up in the morning. 'We went to give her our condolences,' he told his sister, 'and she became very agitated at the news.'[22]

During her days of confinement in the palace, Maria banned all public entertainments and ordered her courtiers to spend most of their time at requiem mass to pray for his soul. On 3 June – her first outing since Pedro's death – she was driven to her convent at Estrela. She had been a regular visitor since the nuns took up residence and had forged a friendship with the abbess, a woman on whom she would become increasingly reliant for spiritual guidance.

She also began to rely more heavily on her confessor, Inácio de São Caetano, who had been given the title of Archbishop of Thessalonica and, alone amongst her subjects, had the privilege of being allowed to sit in her presence. A large, red-faced man who tucked into enormous meals, he was, according to Robert Walpole, 'of a plain, good understanding, with no extensive knowledge beyond his profession but with great influence over Her Majesty in matters of conscience'.

São Caetano was always smiling. 'I never saw a sturdier fellow,' wrote William Beckford. 'He seems to anoint himself with the oil of gladness, to laugh and grow fat.'[23] When Maria confessed that her father's complicity in Pombal's acts of terror lay heavily on her conscience, São Caetano reassured her. 'Be easy concerning your soul,' he said, 'for I shall take that upon myself.'

On 21 June, a special courier arrived from Aranjuez with news of the birth of Maria's first grandchild, a boy named Pedro Carlos. Maria was happy for her daughter but her spirits remained low. She was fifty-one years old, she had lost her husband, and was suffering the hot flushes and mood swings of the menopause. On doctors' advice, she began to take the baths at Alcaçarias.

The baths seemed to calm her so, in early autumn, she set out for Caldas da Rainha where the hot spa waters were thought to be especially beneficial. There was no palace in the town – her grandfather visited Caldas only when his health began to deteriorate; her parents were more interested in hunting than taking the waters – so the house of the *provedor* (the most important man in town) was prepared for her accommodation. This was by no means a palace; when the French ambassador stayed here the following year, he was shocked by the meanness of the apartments. The house was a '*bicoque*,' he wrote in his diary, 'a hovel, by no means suitable for the dignity of the throne of Portugal.'[24]

Maria arrived in Caldas on 9 September to spend her days in the 'large and handsome bathing house' which covered the spa waters in the centre of town. Five weeks later, an Englishman arrived at the *provedor*'s house to present a petition. This was William Stephens who had built the lime kilns near the *Barraca Real*. Thirteen years later, José sent him to rebuild the royal glassworks at Marinha Grande, a village near the royal pine forest, where the Englishman soon transformed a moribund factory into a thriving industrial concern. Stephens had attended court on a number of occasions since Maria came to the throne and now he came to Caldas with a petition about his tax exemptions.

The Englishman had achieved great things at Marinha Grande. Stories were told at court, not only about the volume and quality of his glass, but also about the welfare state he had created in the village. His workers were sober and industrious, his farms produced higher than normal yields, and the people of the region were healthier and better fed than in other parts of the country. He employed teachers of music and dance, and had built a theatre where his workmen acted in plays, many of them by foreign dramatists. A recent production of Voltaire's *Olimpia* was directed by the playwright, Nicolau Luís da Silva, who was – so the court was informed – astonished by the high quality of the performances.

Maria had come to respect William Stephens. He stood out from her priests and courtiers, understated in his dress, restrained in his behaviour, and with a quiet charisma which she found reassuring. She admired his achievements and looked forward to his appearances at court. Marinha Grande lay thirty miles north of Caldas, but only fifteen miles from the convent of Alcobaça where she kept a suite of apartments. She was still in strict mourning for her husband but she was also curious about the glassworks which operated under royal patronage.

On 12 October, when she signed a paper approving his petition, she told Stephens that she would visit his factory five days later. He hurried home to Marinha Grande and, at midday on the 17th, the royal carriages arrived at the glassworks. Maria was the first to alight, followed by her sisters, her two sons and little Carlota who scampered out of the carriage, her short locks hidden beneath a cap. Refreshments were served (lemonade, iced tea and coffee, wine and liqueurs), after which the royal party made a tour of the workshops, rebuilt by Stephens in elegant neoclassical style.

Cooks from Caldas had prepared a *merenda* which was served on the first floor of Stephens's mansion house. After the meal, as the carriages were prepared for departure, Maria told Stephens that she might come again the following year – and according to the *Lisbon Gazette*, the visit was 'all to Her Majesty's satisfaction'.[25]

On 31 October, a few days after Maria's return to Ajuda, a new French ambassador – the Marquis de Bombelles – came to the *Barraca Real* for his first audience with the queen. He kept a private diary and, during the next few months, he recorded the improvement in Maria's spirits. In November, she lifted the ban on public entertainments. In December, she engaged in cheerful conversations with her courtiers. 'Little by little,' he wrote, 'the queen emerges from the profound sadness into which she was plunged by the death of her husband.' By the turn of the year, she was coaching Bombelles in the use of Portuguese phrases.[26]

12

Crisis in Cabinet

The queen is worn out with the intrigues
of the court and sick of her existence.
William Beckford, 22 October 1787

Despite her improved spirits during the winter, Maria was depressed when the court returned to Caldas in May 1787. She stayed in the town for seven weeks, immersing herself in the hot spa waters every day, but she failed to make a second visit to Marinha Grande. Several matters lay heavily on her mind. She was concerned about her daughter in Spain, worried by her elder son's attitude to the church, and unnerved by the need to reorganise her cabinet.

Mariana had inherited her mother's reserve and timidity. She was lonely in the court of Spain and missed the company of her own people. In June, Robert Walpole speculated on the appointment of a new ambassador to Madrid. 'It would be agreeable to the Portuguese Infanta married to Don Gabriel,' he wrote, 'to have an ambassador of this country there, to be frequently in her company to relieve her from the embarrassment to which her natural timidity and taciturnity frequently expose her.'

Prince José also had 'a reserved disposition'. Twenty-seven years old, he was lacking in grace and charm, frustrated at having so little to occupy his time. He would have liked to have succeeded his grandfather (as Pombal had wished him to do) and his secular approach to government was encouraged by some of his courtiers. They suggested that his mother might abdicate and spread rumours that she was thinking of entering a convent.

Meanwhile, the men in Maria's cabinet were ailing. Her secretary of state for foreign affairs, Aires de Sá, had died in May 1786, reducing the number of her ministers to three, two of whom were over seventy and in poor health. The Marquis de Angeja (her first minister) was semi-retired, while Martinho de Melo (her minister of marine and the colonies) was 'subject to frequent and violent attacks of illness which may be attended with the most serious consequences at his advanced age'. After Sá's death, Melo had taken on foreign affairs in addition to his own portfolio and was now handling 'a multiplicity of business which is too much for him'. Maria's third minister, the Viscount de Ponte de Lima (secretary of state for home affairs) was sixty. A deeply religious man, he was inexperienced in government; he was also unwell from time to time, 'afflicted with a fever in his head'.

These matters were preying on Maria's mind when she returned to Lisbon on 26 June, travelling by road to Vila Nova da Rainha and thence by river to the city. Her royal barge, built to celebrate the double marriage in 1785, was a magnificent longboat and she reclined in state in the gilded cabin, 'fanned by refreshing breezes'. She had recently abolished a tax on the sale of *bacalhao* (dried and salted fish) and, as her barge approached Lisbon in the late afternoon, the people of the city gave her a special welcome.

Hundreds of boats 'transformed into arbours of flowers and garlands' had sailed upriver to meet her, some with musicians on board who serenaded Maria during the last leg of the journey. The Praça do Comércio was crowded with people waiting to cheer their sovereign. A carriage was waiting at the quayside but Maria, 'delighted with this demonstration of affection', chose to walk across the square to the Senate House, 'amidst a multitude worked up to the highest pitch of grateful enthusiasm'. 'Such genuine rejoicings,' wrote William Beckford, 'are seldom seen in Portugal and Her Majesty was affected by them almost to tears.'[27]

Cheered by this reception, Maria thought up a solution to the crisis in cabinet. Her elder son needed employment and a role in state affairs. Her confessor had been advising her on matters of government for several years; his understanding of politics was limited but he did have common sense. So on 21 August (the prince's birthday), Maria appointed both Prince José and Inácio de São Caetano to her council of state.

The inclusion of the prince was greeted with satisfaction ('it ought to have been done some years ago') but São Caetano's elevation was met with less enthusiasm. Ponte de Lima tendered his resignation, which Maria refused to accept, and as Melo told Robert Walpole:

> The queen has put her confidence in this person in matters very much out of his sphere of education and intelligence. He has no bad intentions but he is so exceedingly ignorant that, when he cannot be made to comprehend any business beyond his capacity, it becomes an object of conscience for the queen not to adopt it and, of course, many obstacles are thrown in the way to impede or delay matters of consequence and importance.

Maria was distressed by the reaction of her ministers, particularly since they (and Prince José) were treating her confessor with disrespect. She retired to the palace in Sintra for the autumn and, in mid-October, she had a frank conversation with the Marquis de Marialva. And Marialva was indiscreet enough to tell William Beckford. 'He told me in the strictest confidence,' Beckford wrote in his diary, 'that the queen has thoughts of retiring from government, that she is worn out with the intrigues of the court and sick of her existence.'[28]

At the end of the month, Maria returned to the *Barraca Real* where, on 8 November, a special courier arrived from Madrid. Mariana had given birth to her second child, a daughter named Maria. Cannons fired, bells pealed, and in thanksgiving for a safe delivery, the queen ordered the *Te Deum* to be sung in the churches. As dark fell that night, Beckford set out to see the illuminations in the streets. He watched the rockets in the Praça do Comércio (rising to 'a vast height', bursting into 'innumerable blue stars') and returned to his house to find every room 'filled with the thick vapour of wax torches' which his servant had 'set most loyally a-blazing'.[29]

Three days later, a second courier arrived from Madrid, this time with a letter edged in black. Mariana's baby had died on 7 November. The celebrations in Lisbon had taken place when the child was already in her coffin.

On 25 November, Maria attended a performance at the Salitri theatre in Lisbon. Beckford was in the audience, with a good view of the royal box. 'The theatre was uncommonly crowded,' he wrote, 'Her Majesty being there in state with the little Infanta, Dona Carlota, mischievous and full of frolic. The Prince of Brazil and his brother, Dom João, never opened their mouths during the whole performance but to gape. The queen talked a great deal to Marialva. Her manner is uncommonly graceful and dignified.'[30]

Six weeks later, the family set out for Salvaterra. Hunting every day improved Maria's spirits and she was feeling better when she returned to Ajuda in early March. A few days later, the Marquis de Angeja died, reducing the number of her secretaries of state to two. It was vital that she appoint new ministers but, with her usual indecision, she merely asked Ponte de Lima to assume Angeja's role on an interim basis. And for the next nine months, he and the elderly Martinho de Melo conducted all business of state between them.

In early April, a courier arrived from Spain with news that Maria's daughter had conceived for a third time. On the 25th, there was a *beija-mão* to celebrate Carlota's thirteenth birthday. The foreign diplomats attended, all trying to think of a suitable compliment, all lying through their teeth when they congratulated the tiny princess on how much she had grown. 'Such great flattery,' wrote the Marquis de Bombelles, 'was embarrassing to sustain.'[31]

Two weeks later, Maria returned to the *provedor*'s house in Caldas. She was in reasonably high spirits and, when William

Stephens arrived for an audience, she told him she was ready to make another visit to Marinha Grande. She was curious about his theatre and the orchestra he had created from his workforce; she was eager to see his workmen perform on stage. She would arrive, she told him, for a stay of three days.

Maria was an absolute monarch, ruling by divine right. Yet here she was proposing to stay in an industrial complex, to sleep overnight in the house of an Englishman, a man who was not only low-born – the illegitimate son of a servant girl – but also a Protestant, a heretic in the eyes of the Portuguese.

13

English Hospitality

Her Majesty liked her situation so well, she regretted leaving and would have stayed longer had it not been for the unavoidable necessity of returning so soon to Lisbon.
Philadelphia Stephens, 25 July 1788

The royal carriages arrived at the factory gates on 30 June 1788. It was four o'clock in the afternoon and large numbers of people ('an assembly of many thousands') had descended on the village to witness the occasion, 'a vast concourse from all the country around which curiosity had brought together to see their sovereign'.

The glassworkers – almost two hundred men – were drawn up on parade in front of the main workshop, 'their hair dressed and powdered, their shirts clean and ironed, the sleeves tied round the middle with red ribbons, black breeches and clean white stockings, which altogether gave them a very neat appearance'. As the carriages passed through the gates, the men shouted in unison: '*Viva Rainha! Viva toda a Familia Real!*'[32]

William Stephens and his sister Philadelphia were waiting outside the front door of their house which stood to one side of the factory courtyard. With them were Maria's confessor, Inácio de São Caetano, and her secretary of state for home affairs, the Viscount de Ponte de Lima. Maria was the first to alight from her carriage and Philadelphia 'had the honour of kissing Her Majesty's hand and received a gracious smile in return'. She found the queen 'greatly improved in her looks since she was here in the year 1786, being now fatter, of a better colour and more cheerful countenance'.

The greeting ceremony was repeated with each member of the royal family. Prince José was a tallish young man with a pale face and short-sighted air. His wife Benedita was 'short, much inclined to embonpoint, her face handsome, her eyes dark and eloquent'.[33] Mariana, the queen's sister, was 'shorter and thicker' than Maria, 'more agreeable in her countenance, with a ruddy complexion and more animated expression'. Prince João had a pronounced underbite and a habit of keeping his mouth 'somewhat open' as his grandfather used to do. Carlota was 'lively and mischievous'; she had hardly grown since the previous visit in 1786, 'nor does her countenance indicate that she will ever grow much taller. I have seen children as lusty at nine years of age; she is now in her fourteenth.'

São Caetano introduced the ladies-in-waiting to Philadelphia ('recommending them to my particular care'), after which the royal visitors entered the house. Maria inspected the rooms on the first floor – now transformed into royal apartments – before climbing the staircase to the second floor 'to see the accommodations of her female attendants with which she expressed great satisfaction'. She then 'intimated a desire of seeing the fabrick'.

The factory complex was crowded with people as Stephens and Philadelphia led the royal family across the courtyard to the workshops. A pavilion, covered with green baize and crimson taffeta, had been constructed in the largest workshop and Maria stayed here for half an hour, watching the glass-masters wield their blowing rods, their assistants and apprentices busy about them with pincers, scissors and tongs. It was hot so close to the furnace and Benedita, 'afraid of being near the heat so soon after finishing her baths at the Caldas', called to Philadelphia and 'desired I would show her the way upstairs to the packing warehouse ... where she amused herself in admiring the prospect and talking to me in a very agreeable familiar style'.

After 'satisfying her curiosity of seeing the people at work and applauding them all very much', Maria followed her sister upstairs where she 'examined everything very intently'. In the room where the glass was cut and engraved, 'they sat some time admiring the work, the queen and princess both asking a number of questions about our craftsmen'. Finally, 'after taking a view of everything belonging to the fabrick, they walked into the garden where chairs were placed in different situations for them to rest themselves'.

Stephens had spent lavishly on furnishings, decorations and provisions to welcome his illustrious guests. He had acquired 'some hundreds' of beds from the nearby city of Leiria ('it being impossible to collect so great a number in this place'). He had bought fifty yards of velvet, a hundred yards of green and white baize for the dining tables, and four plumes of feathers to decorate the queen's chair.

He had built a marquee in the garden, borrowed houses in the village to accommodate members of the court, provided stabling for almost a thousand horses and mules, and cleared a covered yard to house the servants, coachmen and soldiers of the guard. This was provided with 'kitchens and dining rooms according to their several degrees, a plentiful supply of the best beef, rice and bread that could be got in this country, and as much *Aljubarrota* wine as they chose to drink'. And according to Philadelphia, 'not one got drunk, nor the least disturbance happened during the whole time they were here'.

A few days before the visit, the director of the royal household had arrived in Marinha Grande with 'five beds for the royal family and curtains for the principal rooms'. They hung drapes of deep red damask over the doors and windows, and Philadelphia watched with interest as the servants prepared the beds. José and Benedita shared 'a very large and elegant' bed made of iron gilt. João and Carlota (who still slept in separate rooms) had smaller beds made of brazilwood, Carlota's made up with 'remarkably fine' sheets which she had brought with her from Spain. Philadelphia described Maria's bed in some detail:

> The stands were made of iron gilt, the boards painted white, with a crimson buckram covering and a crimson damask valance. The headboard was covered with crimson damask and bound with silk lace of the same colour. The first mattress was of very fine *pano de linho* which they brought empty and filled here with rye straw. Over this were two mattresses of very fine Irish linen stuffed with wool. These were covered with a very good *pano de linho* sheet which four men pulled with all their strength and tucked in under the straw mattress.
>
> Next was a fine Irish linen sheet tucked in by the same manner. Two flat bolsters were then laid on each other, stuffed with wool and quilted in the same manner as the mattresses. The bolster cases were plain but of finer linen than the sheets. The upper sheet of fine Irish linen was then put on with a crimson damask coverlid. Over this, instead of a blanket, was a white broadcloth covering bound with ribbon. Upon this was another crimson damask coverlid which was also tucked in very tight under the straw mattress, with a deep full flounce that reached from the upper mattress to the floor, the whole trimmed with lace. The state bolster was then laid on the bed and the ends tied with large knots of the best English white ribbon.

On the morning of the visit, Maria's chief cook and 'three and twenty assistant cooks' arrived from Caldas and set to work in the kitchen. Stephens had bought huge quantities of provisions for such an immense gathering. The accounts book at Marinha Grande shows purchases of fat oxen and calves and four hundred gallons of wine:

> Everything was provided so that, on their arrival, the cooks had nothing to do but begin their work. We required nothing from Her Majesty's household but the hangings for the doors and windows and the large coppers for the kitchen. China, damask, table and plate we had sufficient for the service of all the different tables. Having had some reason to expect this

visit last year, we got a large supply of silver-hafted knives and forks and spoons from England, of the best quality and the newest fashion, all of which is carefully preserved for the next occasion, which probably will be next year as the royal family have some thought of going to Coimbra.

Stephens had planned entertainments in the theatre for both evenings of the queen's visit. His workmen were well-rehearsed, his orchestra had been practising every afternoon, and the scenery and costumes were all newly-made.

Maria enjoyed the theatre. 'The Portuguese have so many dramas in their own language,' wrote the Scottish poet, William Julius Mickle. 'Tragedy, comedy, farce, pantomime and pastoral are blended together in every piece I have seen, and a laughing kind of satire, not always very delicate, is the seasoning I particularly relished.'[34] Productions in Lisbon could be crude, the actors suggestive in their movements, so to protect their modesty, Maria had prohibited women from appearing on stage. At first, this had the effect of closing the theatres but they soon reopened, with men and boys playing the female roles.

After the family had taken tea in the house, they walked across the courtyard to the theatre where 'the gallery was elegantly prepared for their reception, being hung with crimson damask, the front ornamented with curtains trimmed with gold lace and hung in festoons, the rails covered with crimson velvet with a deep gold fringe'. As they entered the gallery, the factory orchestra – four violins, two French horns and two violoncellos – began to play the overture.

The performance that night ('by particular desire of Her Majesty') was Maria's favourite play, the tragedy of *Sésostris*. Set in ancient Egypt, this three-act play was often staged in Lisbon. William Beckford had seen a performance in the Salitri Theatre in October 1787 and was not impressed:

A shambling blear-eyed boy dressed in the sable garb of woe squeaked and bellowed the part of a widowed princess.

> Another hobbledehoy tottering on high-heeled shoes represented Her Egyptian Majesty and warbled two airs with all the nauseous sweetness of a fluted falsetto.[35]

Beckford may have disliked the play but the performance at Marinha Grande was, according to Philadelphia, a great success. With only two weeks to learn their lines, 'our young people performed their parts exceeding well'. There were dances and pantomimes between the acts, 'during which the royal family were served with ice of different sorts', and the evening ended with a farce performed to 'great applause'.

After the curtain descended for the last time that night, Stephens and Philadelphia escorted the royal family across the courtyard which was illuminated by two thousand candles strung diagonally across the façades of the buildings. The royal dining table had been set up on the first floor of Stephens's house; it was covered with a pink silk tablecloth and decorated with 'a very elegant glass ornament made here, representing a temple'. The design for the ornament was provided by the Marquis de Marialva's confectioner who also provided the ice creams and sorbets ('of which there was a great variety and exceeding good').

Except for rare occasions, such as the double marriage in Vila Viçosa, the royal family never dined in public ('their usual custom is to sup and dine each in their different apartments'). So Philadelphia, standing in the doorway, watched a protocol that few people had the opportunity to witness. Maria and her sisters sat on one side of the table, her sons on the other, and according to Philadelphia, 'they seemed very happy in each other's company'.

Each member of the family was served separately by their *camarista* (lord of the bedchamber) and *reposteiros* (footmen):

> On the queen's entering the dining room, she is presented by her *camarista* on his knee with water and a towel to wash her hands, which being done she takes her seat and the *camarista* stands behind her chair. The same ceremony is observed with the rest of the royal family. The *camarista* then carves such

dishes as they choose to eat and, when anything is required from the sideboards, the *reposteiros* reach it to the *camarista* who puts it on the table.

When water or wine is required, the *reposteiro* draws the cork and brings the bottle and glass on a salver to the *camarista* who, on his knee, pours out the liquor and presents it to the queen, remaining in the same attitude to receive the glass when she has done drinking. When dinner is over, they again wash their hands and retire to drink coffee.

Even the provision of water had its own ceremonial:

The water is all brought in flasks from Lisbon. One of the *reposteiros* had nothing else to do but keep the key of the water chests and take care that there was always a bottle of water on the sideboard and on a table in each of the apartments. Her Majesty's bottle was distinguished by having some white ribbon tied around the neck.

After the meal, 'some pretty fireworks were displayed off, which amused them about a quarter of an hour'. The family then retired to their rooms and 'a total silence commenced for the night'.

The first to rise next morning was Prince João, who left his bed at four o'clock to visit his estates in Monte Real. By the time he returned four hours later:

The queen and the royal family were up and dressed. They breakfasted in their different apartments on tea and *tosta Inglesa*, after which their travelling altar was erected in the queen's dressing room and mass was celebrated by one of her chaplains. This being over, they amused themselves in walking about the house and conversing very affable with any persons who came their way.

During their previous visit to Marinha Grande, the royal women were dressed in black, still in strict mourning for Pedro. Now they wore 'silk riding habits, every day a different one', with 'velvet girdles around the waist, fastened in front with two large medallions ornamented with steel'. And Maria had 'a little old-fashioned cocked hat which she carries in her hand or under her arm and only puts on her head when she rides on horseback'.

Dinner was served in the house at one o'clock. Once again, Philadelphia watched the proceedings from the doorway and, after the meal, Maria told her that 'she had eaten very hearty, everything being exceeding good'. In the afternoon, the family made an excursion to the city of Leiria, visiting the cathedral, the bishop's palace and a convent of Dominican nuns. They returned to Marinha Grande in time for tea and another evening in the theatre. A comedy ('a laughable piece, acted with great humour') and a farce were performed that night, with more dances and pantomimes. And according to Philadelphia:

> The performers received universal applause, not only from the royal family, but from all the audience who thought it impossible that a rude country place could have produced such good actors. Their surprise was greatly increased on finding that most of them had never been more than two or three leagues from this parish and they all worked in the fabrick. They perform only for their own amusement, which is very different from public theatres where the actors have no other employment than studying their parts.

On the second morning, the royal family rose early. As they dressed, ate breakfast and celebrated mass, horses and mules were brought from the stables, carriages rumbled into the factory courtyard, and servants hurried about attending to the details of departure. José and Benedita were the first to leave, followed an hour later by Maria and the rest of the family who were making a diversion to the fishing village of Nazaré. 'On the queen's leaving her apartment,' wrote Philadelphia, 'I kissed her hand when she thanked me for the entertainment we had given her with a countenance that indicated she was pleased with everything she had seen.'

Maria had enjoyed herself at Marinha Grande. Stephens and his sister had given her a sojourn of simple pleasure, time to relax in congenial surroundings away from the strain of government. 'Her Majesty liked her situation so well,' explained Philadelphia, 'that she regretted leaving and would have stayed longer had it not been for the unavoidable necessity of returning so soon to Lisbon. The orders were already passed for the change of beasts on the road and for everything to be got ready for the reception at the Praça de Comércio, and it was now too late to recede.'

As the royal carriages clattered through the factory gates, as members of the court dispersed for the return journey to Caldas, Stephens congratulated himself on the success of the occasion. 'I went through this affair with great *éclat*,' he told an English visitor. 'It was an honour they have never done any of their own subjects, so I was without a precedent to go by. I requested nothing from the palace but their cooks and the kitchen utensils.'[36]

Philadelphia shared his pride. 'My brother has attained what nobody else in the kingdom can boast of,' she wrote to her cousin in London:

> the honour of entertaining the royal family and all the court for two days and given universal satisfaction to everybody, from the queen down to the scullions and stable boys. The first time of Her Majesty's coming here was not so surprising, as curiosity to see the glass fabrick was supposed to be the motive, but that she should come a second time and sleep two nights in the house of a private person, an Englishman and a Protestant, is a thing that never entered the idea of the Portuguese and has struck all people with amazement.

Part Three

A Fragile Mind

14

A String of Tragedies

Her Majesty bears very strong expressions of affliction in her countenance.
Robert Walpole, 27 September 1788

It was a small party that set out for the fishing village of Nazaré, driving through the dappled shade of the pine forest. Maria stopped to pray at Nossa Senhora de Nazaré, a chapel built to commemorate a foggy day in the 12th century when a man was saved from riding his horse over the cliff by a miraculous appearance of the Virgin. A *merenda* was served in the village, and the family walked down to the sea to watch teams of oxen hauling boats up the beach and women laying the fish out to dry.

Prince José did not accompany his mother on this detour; instead, he and Benedita travelled direct to Caldas, 'being afraid to stop at Nazaré on account of the smallpox there, it being doubtful whether the prince has had this disorder or not'.[1] Prince João, who had suffered a mild attack in 1783, was immune from smallpox but his elder brother had shown no signs of the disease.

Inoculation was discovered in the 1720s and several royal houses had used it to protect their children. The procedure involved inserting a small quantity of pox liquid into the skin of the arm. This resulted in a less severe form of the disease and provided immunity for life, but there were risks involved. The mortality rate was about one in two hundred (Prince Octavius, thirteenth child of George III of England, died from the procedure in 1783). Maria had been advised to inoculate her children but she refused, partly because of the risks involved and partly because of her religious principles. The procedure, she said, was against the will of God.

On 1 September, eight weeks after returning to Lisbon, José began to feel unwell. He complained of pains in his head and back. His temperature began to rise and red spots appeared on his skin. Initially, the doctors were optimistic. 'All the circumstances are favourable,' wrote Robert Walpole on 6 September. 'He is said to have a considerable quantity of pox, but of a good sort.' Maria was confident in the diagnosis and, assuming that José would recover as quickly as João had done in 1783, she continued to go riding in the afternoons.

On 8 September, the doctors changed their minds. The pox blisters had joined up, become confluent. Soon José's nose, mouth and throat were affected. His breathing was laboured, saliva dribbled constantly from his mouth. For the next three days, Maria stayed in the palace, talking with the doctors, praying with her confessor. Her son's condition became critical in the early hours of 11 September. He was given the last rites as dawn broke over the Tagus and died twelve hours later.

Maria remembered the advice to inoculate her children. Distraught with grief, she blamed herself for his death, while her sister Benedita retired to bed 'very much indisposed by this irreparable loss'. As they confined themselves to the *Barraca Real*, the bells of Lisbon tolled day and night, the air reverberating with discharges of artillery. On 14 September, the body was taken to São Vicente de Fora for a state funeral. On the 20th, when the family emerged from their eight-day confinement, the foreign diplomats came to present their condolences. 'Her Majesty bears very strong expressions of affliction in her countenance,' wrote Robert Walpole, 'I think more than upon any former occasion.'

The following day, she fled to Queluz.

José's death had several implications. The first was his widow, Benedita, who had lost the prospect of becoming queen-consort and now had to give precedence to a tiny thirteen-year-old child. The first time the family attended chapel after José's death, 'an affecting scene was displayed, a contest accompanied by tears and expressions of grief', as Carlota went through the motions of insisting that her sister-in-law retain her precedence. Maria grieved for Benedita but she had to enforce the rules of etiquette. A few days later, when she settled 100,000 *cruzados* a year on her widowed sister, she was 'so much affected that she could hardly go through this afflicting ceremony'.

A second problem was the rumour that José had been allowed to die by an establishment troubled by his liberal ideas. During his time as the prince's preceptor, Cenáculo Vilas Boas had instilled enlightened opinions in his pupil. He had taught him law and political history, and it was known that José was in favour of 'more sober and beneficial public regulations' instead of (in Walpole's words) 'the pompous, vain and expensive establishment of the patriarchal church'. As the envoy put it:

> It is suspected that His Royal Highness was very unskilfully treated. The nobility are cautious and prudent and silently lament the late melancholy event, but the imprudent lower class have not refrained from reflecting upon the ignorance and unskilfulness of the principal physician. This having reached Her Majesty's ears may have contributed to her resolution to retire to Queluz.

A third worry was the future of the monarchy. José's marriage had produced no children; João's marriage was still unconsummated and there was concern about Carlota's fertility. The Marquis de Bombelles (who called Carlota 'an embryo' in the private pages of his diary) wrote that her restricted growth was an abnormality in an already defective family, 'more bad blood poured into narrow veins'.[2]

The issue was more serious than the matter of children alone, for Bombelles also noted that João was angry, 'annoyed at having resigned himself to marrying this stunted princess, this little spider monkey'.[3] Walpole tried to put it more delicately:

> I avoid troubling you with the private speculations of some, or the greater freedom in language of others, with regard to what may be – or ought to be – in contemplation upon the future fate of the Spanish Infanta, Dona Carlota, as a subject of too delicate a nature, even for the most sincere well-wisher to the prosperity of this country.

He not only referred to the 'great improbability' of Carlota bearing children, he also mentioned the 'dislike which the prince, her husband, may be disposed to have towards her'. Portugal might ask for an annulment, he wrote, so Carlota could be sent back to Spain.

There was a precedent for this. In 1722, Maria's mother had been betrothed to Louis XV of France at the age of three. She went to live in the French court and remained there until 1725 when it was thought expedient for Louis (aged fifteen and in frail health) to beget an heir as soon as possible. Mariana was returned to Madrid. The consequence was a political rift between the two countries and Walpole was concerned that a request for Carlota's return would have the same result, a breach with Spain which Maria would find distressing. It was she who had nurtured good relations with her uncle Charles III, she who had arranged the details of the marriage. Her ministers may have discussed the idea amongst themselves; it is unlikely they were brave enough to bring it to her attention.

Maria remained in seclusion at Queluz for almost three months. On 4 November, she was heartened by the arrival of a special courier from Madrid with news that her daughter had given birth to a second son on 31 October. But Mariana was running a fever when she gave birth and soon the familiar red spots appeared on her skin. For the next two days, as the spots turned into pimples and the pimples into blisters, special couriers left Madrid with the latest news. Finally, on 6 November, Maria received a letter from her uncle. 'What I feared so much has happened,' he wrote, 'the loss of our Mariana. It grieves me to send you this terrible news.'[4]

This second tragedy caused Maria, as Walpole put it, 'a considerable degree of affliction', grief which deepened four days later when another letter arrived from her uncle in Spain:

> In all my life I have never felt so sad. The day before yesterday, the doctors found smallpox in our newborn grandson, a disease he brought with him from his unfortunate mother's womb. It seems the pox is benign, but God knows whether such a tender child will overcome this terrible malady.[5]

The infant died that same evening. Seventeen days later, his father Gabriel died from the same disease.

Maria received the news of Gabriel's death on 27 November. The following day, Inácio de São Caetano – the confessor on whom she placed her entire trust and confidence – suffered a massive stroke in the palace at Queluz. He was seventy years old, and as he lay dying, he asked Maria's pardon 'for any harm he may have caused her, for any discredit he may have brought upon her'.[6]

In the space of seven weeks, Maria had lost two of her three surviving children, as well as her main pillar of strength and support. Alone amongst her advisers, São Caetano had the ability to soothe her troubled mind. His death, as Walpole put it, was 'a serious loss to the queen for she had put her confidence in this person for a considerable number of years and permitted her conscience to be guided by him since her accession to the throne'. Maria would, he continued, 'be directed in her choice of a new confessor' by the abbess of the convent in Estrela, 'who, for many years, has had a considerable share of Her Majesty's confidence'.

Charles III was old and tired when he informed Maria about the death of her son-in-law. 'Gabriel has died,' he wrote. 'I shall follow him soon.'[7] A chill turned into a fever and Charles died on 14 December, the sixth death in three months.

Two days later, Maria raised the strength to appoint two additional secretaries of state. This had become a matter of urgency since the Marquis de Angeja died in March, leaving the cabinet in the hands of two ministers (Martinho de Melo and Ponte de Lima), both of whom were 'overloaded with business'. Now some fresh blood entered the cabinet. Luís Pinto de Sousa Coutinho (who had recently served as Portuguese ambassador in London) was appointed secretary of state for foreign affairs, and José de Seabra e Silva (the minister exiled by Pombal) took over home affairs, leaving Ponte de Lima to run the treasury and act as Maria's first minister.

The delay in making these appointments was partly due to Maria's indecision and partly the result of a disagreement between São Caetano and Prince José. São Caetano had been lobbying for the inclusion of Seabra but José held a grudge against him ('the prince is not favourably disposed towards that gentleman'), no doubt resenting his intervention in 1774 which may have cost him the throne. Now, with both José and São Caetano in their graves, the abbess at Estrela had taken up the matter. As Walpole explained:

> The sudden resolution in favour of these two gentlemen has been a complete defeat to the nobility who had planned for themselves the different departments of government. The measure is said to be a request of the late confessor and has been accomplished by the means of the abbess.

The reorganisation was greeted with dismay in the cabinet. Martinho de Melo responded to the inclusion of Seabra 'in a very unrestrained manner, indicating that he could not co-operate with that gentleman; he also declined being present when Monsieur de Seabra took his place at the council'. As a result, Maria decided 'that each secretary of state shall have a separate day for dispatching business, which will prevent any altercation in her presence'. Melo continued to complain. 'He is still very much dissatisfied,' wrote Walpole, 'and pleads his age and ill-state of health as motives for wishing Her Majesty to dispense with his service.'

15

On the Brink

Her Majesty does not think herself perfectly well.
She complains of pains in her stomach and want of sleep.
Robert Walpole, 12 November 1791

On 17 December 1788, Maria held an official audience in the *Barraca Real* to celebrate her fifty-fourth birthday. During the audience, she and Robert Walpole discussed her new secretaries of state, particularly Luís Pinto who had impressed the British government during his years in London. They also spoke of the mental health of George III who was suffering his first attack of dementia (a symptom of porphyria which the doctors mistook for madness). The illness had first appeared in November and George was in the care of Francis Willis, a doctor who specialised in treatment of the insane. During her conversation with Walpole, Maria 'expressed her concern for His Majesty and sent sincere wishes for a speedy re-establishment of his health'.

This conversation was a poignant one, for Maria herself was on the cusp of insanity. Her grandfather, Philip V of Spain, and her uncle, Ferdinand VI, both suffered from mental illness and both had lost all reason by the end of their lives. There are many parallels between their symptoms and Maria's condition which began to appear at about this time.

Philip believed that fire was consuming him from the inside, divine punishment for his mortal sins. His moods swung between extreme lethargy and outbursts of violent frenzy. He screamed and howled for hours at a time, he sang aloud and bit himself. He refused to have his beard shaved or his hair and toenails cut. He believed himself unable to walk because his feet were of different sizes.

Ferdinand inherited his father's illness. He lived in fear of sudden death, convinced his body was being destroyed from the inside, that he would die if he lay down. He refused to be washed, shaved or dressed. He refused food, taking liquid refreshment only. He banged his head against the wall and attacked his servants. In a manic phase, he would spend ten days or more without sleep. At other times, he would collapse into lethargy, becoming completely inert.

This was the illness that lay in wait for Maria. The recent tragedies were too much for her fragile mind to bear, while the abbess did the queen no favours in recommending her nephew, José Maria de Melo (the thirty-year-old Bishop of Algarve) to the post of her confessor. Inácio de São Caetano had made light of the horrors of hell; he had kept Maria on a reasonably even keel. Her new confessor was the worst possible choice.

Appointed to the post on 5 December, the bishop was described by Walpole as 'very devout and retired from the world', and by William Beckford as a young-looking man 'whose small, sleek, school-boyish head and sallow countenance were overshadowed by an enormous pair of green spectacles'. Beckford also referred to 'an expression which did not absolutely partake of the most decent, mild or apostolic character'.[8] Related to the nobility, the bishop put pressure on Maria to rehabilitate families implicated in the Távora conspiracy. At the same time, he enjoyed preaching about the terrors of hell and gave his queen no comfort, preferring to heighten her dread of hellfire which, he told her, was waiting for her just around the corner.

For more than thirty years, Maria had agonised over her father's complicity in the persecution of so many of his subjects. Now, traumatised by grief, she was convinced his soul would suffer eternal damnation. There was nothing she could do to repair the damage, so she came to believe that she too was damned and would burn forever in the infernal flames.

Maria's mental state was growing increasingly fragile but, despite anxieties and night panics, she retained a grip on reality for most of the next three years. She was sometimes 'indisposed', unable to meet with her secretaries of state, but she managed to cope with many of her public appearances.

In January 1789, she left Lisbon for Salvaterra where she spent several weeks in the hunting park. In April, she 'testified her joy' at the recovery of George III and attended a *Te Deum* in a convent of English nuns. In June, she watched the army on manoeuvres near Queluz, but she never made the planned journey to Coimbra. She never returned to Marinha Grande where Stephens's silver-hafted cutlery remained in its boxes.

In early July, the outbreak of the French Revolution gave rise – as Walpole put it – to 'much seriousness at court'. A few weeks later, Prince João became ill with fever and 'a considerable swelling of the parotid glands'. This was an attack of mumps and it caused 'a good deal of uneasiness, chiefly on account of the particular situation of this royal family'. The future of the Bragança monarchy was at risk, not only because of João's illness, but also because of Carlota's doubtful fertility. So Maria's ministers hatched a plan to bring her only grandchild, Pedro Carlos, to Lisbon. 'There seems to be nothing left for the security and tranquillity of this country,' Luís Pinto told Walpole, 'than to bring the prince to Portugal.'

First child of Gabriel and Mariana, Pedro Carlos was a Bourbon but, if the fundamental law against foreign princes was repealed and the boy was brought up in the Portuguese court, the people might – if João and Carlota failed to have children – accept him as their sovereign. The new king of Spain, Charles IV, agreed. The boy, now three years old, would set out for the border in October with the extended name of Pedro Carlos de Bourbon e Bragança.

By the end of August, João was feeling better and Maria ordered celebrations to mark his recovery. A few days later, she moved to Queluz. She was troubled by the events in France which the *Lisbon Gazette* was reporting in colourful detail.

Terrified that the mob might also rise in Portugal, she banned the editor from publishing any further bulletins from Paris ('which have produced some shrewd observations from the lower class of persons here').

In October, Maria's grandson arrived in Portugal, received at the border by the Marquis of Marialva who accompanied him in Lisbon. The first time the child appeared in public, Maria ordered that all members of the court should kiss his hand in submission. 'It may not be improper to observe,' commented Walpole, 'that this intimation has not been received without being silently criticised.' One courtier avoided the issue by lifting up the boy in his arms and kissing his cheek instead.

Meanwhile, Maria's church in Estrela had finally been completed. Constructed of white limestone, the interior lined in geometric patterns of different coloured marbles, it was built at enormous expense, estimated by Walpole at 'not much less than a million sterling'. On 15 November 1789, the church was consecrated 'with great solemnity' in the presence of the royal family and the court. It was a painful occasion for Maria who had commissioned the church in thanksgiving for the birth of Prince José. Now both her husband and her son lay in the mausoleum at São Vicente de Fora.

Four months later, Carlota experienced her first period, a loss of blood which led to much rejoicing. 'It is a matter of great joy and satisfaction to this court,' wrote Walpole on 24 March 1790, 'that the state of nubility of the Infanta Dona Carlota is no longer doubtful. It is therefore decided that she is to cohabit with the Prince of Brazil about the 25th of next month, her birthday.' But João was unwilling to wait, so Maria brought the date forward. As she wrote to Carlota's mother (Queen Maria Luísa) in Spain:

> Our beloved Carlota has reached full womanhood without the slightest trouble. Even before this, I was intending to let them get together, however briefly, as she was so well-informed about everything and João was so keen for

> conjugal relations. Now we are beyond doubt, it will happen over Easter and I feel great happiness.[9]

On the night of 5 April, Maria undressed Carlota and placed her in the marriage bed. She waited until João arrived, prayed with them for the success of their union, then left the room. It was an occasion which João had been anticipating for almost five years. He and Carlota had grown to dislike each other, but he still wanted to 'play with' his young wife. Next morning, Maria wrote another letter to Maria Luísa: 'Our beloved Carlota joined herself with her husband yesterday. They spent the night together well and are very happy.'[10]

'The king and queen of Spain,' wrote Walpole three weeks later, 'were extremely pleased at the consummation of the marriage, for which that court had shown an impatience bordering on indecency.'

Meanwhile, events in France continued to weigh on Maria's mind and she asked Luís Pinto to arrange for confidential dispatches to be sent from Paris. And as the news worsened, every report of mob violence, every example of disrespect to the French royal family, filled her with dread. In March 1790 – in a reversal of her previous policy – she agreed to the public execution of three men convicted of 'burglary and assassinations'. Crowds of people ('unaccustomed to scenes of this kind in late years') flocked into the main square of Lisbon to watch the event. It was a gruesome sight and, as an English spectator put it, 'many of them had to repent their curiosity'.[11]

In May, army manoeuvres were held near Ajuda and the royal family 'amused themselves by reviewing the infantry'. In October, Maria was 'indisposed' and delayed her return from Queluz to Lisbon. In December, she reduced the number of her official audiences. She also signed an edict lifting the mark of infamy on the Duke de Aveiro's son (who had been reduced to penury because of his family's disgrace), an occasion which triggered another attack of hysteria. In January 1791, she was rowed upstream to Salvaterra and Walpole assured the British government that she was 'in perfect good health'.

Six months later, news arrived in Queluz that Louis XVI and his family had been captured while trying to flee the country and were now imprisoned in the Tuileries. Maria was aghast ('considerably affected') and ordered that two million *cruzados* be sent from state reserves 'to the service of the French king's cause'.

In August, she spent two weeks at Mafra where she laid the foundation stone of a new convent for Franciscan friars. Despite eighteen months of sharing a bed with Prince João, Carlota had failed to conceive and the stone was inscribed with a dedication to St Anthony: 'in hopes of the continuance of the progeny of the royal family'.

On 28 September, she attended the launch of a frigate. A few days later, 'she began to sink into a great melancholy, with night-time distress, interrupted sleep and a sinking of the spirits'.[12] In early November, she returned to the *Barraca Real* but failed to appear at official audiences. At the end of the month, with masterly understatement, Walpole reported that 'Her Majesty does not think herself perfectly well. She complains of pains in her stomach and want of sleep'.

16

A Private Hell

Her Majesty was firmly persuaded that she was in hell, saying that a skilful physician may sometimes cure madness, but could never reverse the decrees of fate.
Attributed to Dr Francis Willis, c.1792

Throughout December, Maria remained 'very low-spirited' and the doctors were called to 'consult upon the causes of her uneasiness and apprehensions'. On 4 January, she was 'blooded', a procedure she found distressing. 'She was very averse to it,' wrote Walpole, 'and does not allow that she was in the least relieved by it.' João made plans to take her to Salvaterra, to separate her from the abbess in Estrela to whom she was making 'frequent and long' visits and returning full of gloom, suffering from 'melancholy reflections, uneasiness in her head and her mind very much afflicted'.

The winter rains had arrived with violence and the departure for Salvaterra was postponed several times before the family finally embarked on 14 January. Two weeks later, Walpole reported that 'the queen's health has not received any advantage from her removal to Salvaterra where the rains, which have continued since her arrival there, must have rendered that residence very unhealthy as well as inconvenient'.

Maria was now in great distress. Her confessor, the Bishop of Algarve, continued to put pressure on her to rehabilitate families implicated in the Távora conspiracy and, after her arrival at Salvaterra, he produced a paper for her to sign. 'This made a deep impression on her mind,' explained Walpole. 'She became very much indisposed towards her confessor, and he fell sick and was blooded in consequence of it.'

This reminder of her father's complicity in Pombal's reign of terror was too much for Maria's fragile mind to bear. To the horror of her family, she began to 'rant and rage', with only occasional 'moments of lucidity and coherent speech'. The doctors were called from Lisbon and, by the end of January, it was decided that 'Her Majesty should return to Lisbon to take the baths of Alcaçarias'. On the evening of 2 February, Maria was calm enough to attend an opera in the theatre but she broke down completely during the performance, throwing a fit far worse than any she had suffered in recent days. Lifted up bodily, she was carried into her bedroom where she screamed and howled through the night.

Early next morning, she was led on board the royal barge. During the next few hours, the rhythm of the oars, the creaking of timbers, the sound of rain falling on water, all helped to calm her distress. She was 'in a tranquil state' when the barge arrived at the Praça do Comércio, where she was hustled into a carriage for the short journey across the square to the Senate House. Soon afterwards, 'she appeared at a window of the palace which looks into the square where a considerable number of persons were assembled and saw her'.

Since October, the doctors had given out that Maria had no 'serious or alarming disorder' but, by the evening of 4 February, 'the government could no longer conceal the real state of the queen's health'. All public entertainments were cancelled, prayers were intoned in the churches and convents, and sacred images were carried in procession to the Senate House. Luís Pinto, Maria's secretary of state for foreign affairs, wrote to the Portuguese ambassador in London:

> It is with great sadness that I inform you that Her Majesty is suffering from a melancholic affliction which has descended into insanity, into what is feared to be a total frenzy. In view of this unfortunate situation, I believe it would be helpful for

> Dr Willis, the principal doctor who assisted His British Majesty in similar circumstances, to come to this court as soon as possible. You will provide him with all the money he might request, with no limitations. You will agree to all he proposes, should you enter into a contract with him, and will leave the remuneration to the generous discretion of this court.

He continued by giving the background to Maria's illness:

> The queen has always been of a gloomy temperament and subject to nervous afflictions. Her disposition is one of great meekness and a certain shyness, her imagination vivid, her habits inclined towards spirituality. For years she has suffered from stomach ailments and spasms of the abdomen, which are worsened by the aversion she has to purgative medicines, especially enemas to which she would never consent.[13]

During the next few weeks, Maria's behaviour swung between extreme lassitude ('she appears dead at times and cannot be roused at all') and violent excitement ('almost constant delirium'). She was bled again on 11 February. She was taken to the baths at Alcaçarias and struggled violently as she was placed in the water ('with a force greater than could naturally have been expected').

She complained of uneasiness in her head, pains in her stomach, and 'an impediment in her throat which prevents her swallowing'. She refused to eat at mealtimes ('though, in the course of the day, she eats as it were by stealth what is placed in different parts of the room'). She refused to take medicine so, despite her protests, the doctors held her down and administered enemas. She dismissed the royal musicians who had been playing 'in a room separated from her room by a thin partition', alleging that it was 'improper to have music while prayers and processions are observed for the recovery of her health'. She remained awake at night, screaming in fear and distress.

Religion – and fear of damnation – caused her the greatest anguish. Sometimes she was quieter, with 'intervals of reminiscence and reasonable talk', but she became agitated if she was taken to chapel or saw a religious procession from the windows of the palace. And when she did speak coherently, 'she returns to the first idea that afflicted her, that she is condemned, that there is no help for her salvation'.[14]

The abbess in Estrela wrote to the Pope, asking for dispensation to leave the convent and visit the queen, an offer which Prince João had the sense to refuse. At the same time, Maria's ministers were begging him to take charge of affairs of state in his mother's name. João had received little useful education. He was shy, timid and indecisive, and he found it impossible to conquer what Walpole referred to as 'his respect and condescension to the queen'. He agreed to the ministers' request on 10 February but was unwilling to pick up the reins of government. As a result, no state business could be dispatched for several months.

Meanwhile, the ambassador in London was negotiating with Dr Francis Willis, on whom the entire country rested its hopes. Willis ran a private lunatic asylum in Lincolnshire. He had been called to treat George III in December 1788 and his reputation was greatly enhanced when the king recovered his senses a few months later. Now he was summoned to Lisbon and paid £20,000 to treat the queen of Portugal.

Willis had some psychological insight, but treatments of the mentally ill were brutal at the time and he favoured the strait-jacket, coercion, blistering, and water baths. A man with little self-doubt, he insisted on complete physical and mental domination over his patients. He arrived in Lisbon on 15 March and soon discovered that Maria's condition – a rare and particularly severe form of bi-polar disease – was not susceptible to his 'scientific' treatments. She herself held this view, telling Dr Willis that she was in hell, 'that a skilful physician may sometimes cure madness but could never reverse the decrees of fate'.[15]

At the doctor's suggestion, the royal family moved to Queluz. It was more peaceful in the countryside and Maria could be taken into the grounds away from public scrutiny. Dr Willis also hoped to remove her from the courtiers and secretaries of state (Marialva and Ponte de Lima being two of the worst offenders) who were encouraging her to attend mass, say prayers and sing the *Te Deum*, forms of worship which only served to excite her. 'Whether the doctor will succeed in this part of his recommendation is very doubtful,' wrote Walpole, 'considering the difficulty of changing the customs of etiquette of this court.' Protocol demanded that courtiers pay their respects to the queen every day and Prince João was too timid and immature to direct otherwise.

Another regular visitor was Maria's confessor, the Bishop of Algarve, who was, according to Walpole, 'exceedingly distressed in regard to the scruples of his office'. When his behaviour at Salvaterra became public knowledge, he found himself blamed for the queen's 'alienation of mind'. He was insulted in the streets and treated at court with 'very little respect'. Dr Willis denied him access to the queen, so he lurked about the antechambers, engaging her ladies-in-waiting in earnest conversations.

Maria's condition continued to deteriorate. Sometimes she was violent and distressed ('returned to her state of despair upon the subject of her salvation'). Sometimes she was more cheerful ('in a humour of singing which I doubt very much is a favourable symptom'). Now Willis began to use his more cruel treatments. She was constrained in a straitjacket; she had blistering ointments applied to her legs; she was immersed in ice-cold baths, a procedure 'which occasioned a considerable amount of resistance and was followed by an aguish fever and a great deal of agitation'. To rid her body of evil humours, she was given enemas and emetics, and because she refused to eat, an instrument was made 'for the conveying of nourishment down her throat'.

The doctor may have used brutal methods, but he understood – in a way that no member of the court was willing to accept – that her condition was exacerbated by religious imagery.

He was unable to prevent 'the bustle and preparations' for the Corpus Christi procession at Queluz and soon realised that his only hope was to remove the queen from the source of her terror. The journey downriver from Salvaterra had calmed her agitation. She had also ('after some opposition') allowed João to take her sailing on the river and was 'pretty quiet' on board the royal yacht. So in mid-June, Willis recommended a sea voyage.

This proposal led to a misunderstanding. While the doctor's intention was to remove Maria from the vast numbers of people who surrounded her, João simply assumed that the government and the entire court would embark with her. He ordered several ships to be fitted out for the purpose. When Willis explained that this was not what he had in mind, ministers, nobles and priests were all asked for their opinion. Most of them raised objections, while 'some persons contributed to alarm Her Majesty upon the dangers of going to sea, exciting in her an aversion and opposition which she had never discovered till lately'.

On 8 July, Maria's 'apprehensions were so much increased that a very severe fever ensued and afflicted her during the whole night'. Next morning, the plan was abandoned and Dr Willis resigned. He would return to England at the end of the month. Before he left, he asked Maria a few probing questions:

> He endeavoured by his conversations with the queen to discover whether her malady is not occasioned by political as well as religious motives. She answered that it was a matter of the greatest secrecy. He asked her whether any paper which related to the noblemen of a passed period had been produced for her to sign. She answered in the negative. He then asked her why she had forbidden the confessor to appear in her presence, to which she remained silent. After reflecting on this conversation, she appeared to be uneasy at having gone too far and said too much.

Maria was distressed that the doctor was leaving. He had gained her confidence and she was 'persuaded that she shall grow worse when he shall have left the country'. As indeed she did. She became increasingly obstinate ('she is more intractable and makes difficulties on the smallest trifles'). In August, 'upon a desire to hear mass at an unusual hour, she was carried to chapel but behaved in a very extravagant manner and has since been so very much disturbed that her attendants have been obliged to use constraint'. By September (at a time when Carlota was 'showing favourable symptoms of pregnancy'), she was 'declining towards a state of childishness'.

João appointed a new doctor from Coimbra, a man with no experience of mental illness, and Maria sank further into her private world of despair. In March the following year, when she had been moved to the *Barraca Real*:

> Her Majesty is in a most melancholy state. Her memory seems to have left her and she has but a confused idea of persons and things. She has lately had a very bad disorder in one of her eyes which threatened to be of a gangrenous nature. An operation has been made, with success as to the cure but possibly fatal as to the sight.

Her ministers gave up any hope of recovery. They tried to persuade João to accept the regency but the prince was too frightened. He continued to make decisions in his mother's name and it was not until July 1799 (after 'the long experience of seven years in which the care and assistance of the most able physicians have been of no effect') that he finally agreed to the title of regent.

Carlota's first child was born at Queluz on 29 April 1793, ending the speculation about the future of the Bragança monarchy. João ordered the usual celebrations in Lisbon – bells, cannon-fire and illuminations – and planned great festivities at Queluz. There were bullfights and jousting, displays of shifting lights, and an illuminated air balloon that – released from the gardens – rose into the night sky until it disappeared from sight.

The following summer, Walpole wrote that Maria remained 'in the same unfortunate state of mind, frequently very fretful, very much disposed to a perfect indifference to everything, and dreading every incitement to exertion'. And now her sister, Mariana, began to show signs of the same disease ('afflicted with the same melancholy disorder'), the third of José's four daughters to fall prey to this distressing inheritance. Only Benedita retained her sanity.

The family spent the summer and autumn of 1794 in Queluz, returning to the *Barraca Real* on 8 November, a long train of carriages and carts bringing the royal furniture and furnishings to Ajuda. Two days later, a fire broke out in a servant's room. The alarm was raised at eight o'clock in the evening and 'the flames spread so rapidly that the whole family was obliged to make their escape in the greatest haste'. Maria remained remarkably calm as she was taken 'to a place of safety at a little distance'. Benedita walked quietly to a nearby house 'on the arm of one of the helpers in the kitchen'. Only Mariana showed distress, becoming 'exceedingly violent in an increased paroxysm of the disorder', biting and scratching the men who led her to safety.

By ten o'clock, 'the whole edifice was in a blaze', and João and Carlota stood in the gardens, watching the flames devour the wooden building which had served as the royal palace for almost forty years. 'The jewels,' wrote the British consul, 'with most of the plate, the papers and part of the library, some wearing apparel and a very small portion of the furniture, are the only things saved.' Later that night, the royal carriages returned to Queluz. The servants hurried about making the family as comfortable as possible but, since their beds and furnishings had been consumed in the fire, 'the royal personages suffered considerable inconvenience'.

After the fire, João ordered that a new palace should be built at Ajuda (a palace which took several decades to complete). He and his family took up official residence at Queluz where William Beckford, on his second visit to Portugal, was given a graphic description of Maria's condition:

> Her sufferings are frightfully severe. This very evening, the prince knelt by her couch above two hours, whilst in a

> paroxysm of mental agony, she kept crying out for mercy, imagining that, in the midst of a raging flame which enveloped the whole chamber, she beheld her father's image a calcined mass of cinder, in colour black and horrible. This vision haunts her by night and by day.[16]

In Maria's imagination – which she perceived as truth – she could see her father burning in hell. This fate awaited Maria too and Beckford heard the sounds of shrieking. 'Ai Jesus! Ai Jesus!' she cried, the sounds echoing through the gilded rooms of the palace.

17

The Gathering Storm

Don't drive so fast! People will think we are fleeing.
Maria I, 27 November 1807

A pavilion had been completed at Queluz in 1789, originally intended to house the apartments of José and Benedita. After the loss of the *Barraca Real*, it became Maria's place of confinement. She no longer appeared in public and lived in seclusion with her servants and attendants. Every day, she was taken into the gardens for fresh air and exercise, and travellers between Lisbon and Sintra – who could look down into the palace grounds from an adjacent hill – sometimes saw her there, her long white hair hanging loose around her shoulders.

Carlota proved her fertility during the next eleven years by giving birth to a further eight children – not all of them fathered by her husband. She also grew into a malicious, vindictive woman who hated her husband for his lethargy and indecision. On his part, João avoided his wife's company and, by 1806, they were living apart, he at Mafra, she in Queluz or in her country house at Sintra. And by this time, Portugal was in great political danger.

The French Revolution, which caused such dread in Maria's mind, led to the outbreak of war in April 1792, three months after Prince João took responsibility for affairs of state. Following his mother's example, he declared a state of 'the most perfect neutrality', but after Britain entered the war in February 1793, he agreed to provide 'mutual aid' during the hostilities. The most important aid that Portugal could offer its oldest ally was a safe harbour at Lisbon, so the closure of Portuguese ports to British shipping became an important objective in French military strategy.

Maria had done little to improve the country's defences. João did little to prepare for the coming hostilities. Apart from a few new battleships and some military manoeuvres, he made no preparations for war, no contingency plans for invasion. His lack of education, limited intelligence and indecisive personality left him paralysed in an increasingly dangerous situation. 'No-one doubts the natural good qualities of the Prince of Brazil,' wrote a visitor to Portugal, 'but his talents are questionable and it is feared that he will not escape the yoke of the priesthood by whom his mother is so much oppressed. He has no striking passions or inclinations, except perhaps that for the chase.'[17]

In August 1796, Spain entered the war as an ally of France. Four months later, a British squadron arrived in the Tagus, under the command of Admiral Sir John Jervis, with orders to report on the country's naval defences. Jervis was unimpressed. 'The arsenal is unprovided,' he wrote to the Admiralty, 'owing to the neglect of the late minister of marine, the bad state of finances, and the supineness of the government which exhibits the most melancholy picture. No reliance whatever can be placed on the Portuguese marine for the defence of the nation.' He had no better news about the army. 'I doubt whether they could bring more than twelve thousand into the field,' he wrote, 'and these would be without any necessary provision in opening a campaign, neither hospitals nor hospital staff, camp equipage or clothing except what they have on their backs.'[18]

In early 1801, Prince João received an ultimatum from France. If he wished to remain in peace, he must close his ports to British vessels; if he failed to comply, he must face invasion. João refused the ultimatum. A Franco-Spanish force crossed the border in May and Portugal capitulated two weeks later. This was an ignominious defeat but, when England and France signed an armistice in October, it seemed that the war was over.

Lisbon rejoiced too soon. The war resumed in 1803 and, when Spain re-entered hostilities in 1805, Portugal was once again in danger. The closure of its ports to British shipping was of renewed importance in French military strategy. Pulled by Britain and France in different directions, the weak and frightened Prince João did his best to please both sides. For a short time in early 1806, he fell ill from stress, suffering from anxiety, faintness and poor memory. He complained of chasms opening in the ground beneath his feet and it was feared that he too might be going insane, a fear fostered by Carlota who was plotting to take over the regency.

In August 1806, another squadron commanded by Sir John Jervis (now Lord St Vincent) arrived in Lisbon, this time with a mission to ascertain whether Portugal had any intention or capacity to defend itself – and if not, to persuade the royal family to sail for safety in Brazil. St Vincent did not mince his words. 'The army is very much diminished since I was last in Portugal,' he wrote. 'Thirteen thousand ill-armed infantry is the most that can be counted upon and the cavalry beggars description, both as to horses and men.'[19]

João was terrified at the idea of sailing for Brazil, of leaving the only country he had ever known. 'The reluctance to remove was universal and deep-rooted,' wrote the secretary to the mission. 'Those at the head of affairs plainly showed us that no result of invasion would be more hateful than banishment across the Atlantic to those whose excursions had hitherto been confined to a journey between their town and country residence at home.'[20]

Great parties were held on the flagship while the squadron was in the Tagus. 'We were in perpetual masquerade the whole time,' wrote St Vincent, 'not less than a thousand Portuguese on board every day. All the ministers, domestic and foreign, dined on board, except the Spanish and French. The principal nobility also dined on board and we had very pretty dances, Captain Ricketts having the best taste for turning a quarter-deck into a ballroom that I ever saw.'[21]

The squadron left Lisbon in October, having concluded that Portugal was unable to defend itself and that no British force of any practicable size could prevent an invasion. A few weeks later, Napoleon issued the Berlin Decree which closed the ports of continental Europe to British vessels. This was an effective blockade of Britain and her colonies, and João came under increasing pressure to close his ports. At the same time, British officials were urging him to seek safety in Brazil. João felt himself pulled this way and that. To appease France, he sometimes pretended that he had a mind to close his ports; to appease England, he indicated that he might leave the country.

In July 1807, France issued another ultimatum. Portugal must close its ports to British vessels or face invasion. And while João continued to prevaricate, an invasion force gathered in Bayonne. The British envoy did his best to persuade the prince to leave the country but, as João put it, 'every feeling of religion and duty forbids me to abandon my people until the last moment'.[22]

On 1 October, when the French and Spanish ministers left the country, João referred to his 'well-grounded hopes that their absence will be temporary and that no hostile act will follow'. It was only when he was shown an announcement in a Paris newspaper ('the House of Bragança has ceased to reign') that he realised the full gravity of the situation. He closed his ports on 20 October but it was too late. The invasion force had crossed into Spain two days earlier, with orders to march on Lisbon and seize the royal family.

The Portuguese fleet was anchored in the Tagus. On 17 November, a British squadron arrived to escort the royal family to Brazil but João continued to wait, still refusing to leave until the last possible moment. On 22 November, news arrived that the invading army had crossed into Portugal; two days later, it had reached Abrantes, less than sixty miles from the city. Only now did João make the painful decision. It was time to leave.

The next two days were filled with intense activity. The royal family, the aristocracy, secretaries of state, ministers and officials, their families, friends and servants, all were sailing for Brazil, leaving behind a council of regents nominated by Prince João to rule the country in his absence. The palace of Queluz was packed up in great disorder. Furniture and luggage were piled up in the rain, the royal carriages 'drove about aimlessly, abandoning the protocol usually accorded to these occasions'.[23] Maria's attendants stripped the pavilion. Her furniture and furnishings, her pictures and hangings, the black silk dresses in her wardrobe, were on their way to Brazil.

The royal family boarded ship on the morning of 27 November. Rain had been falling for several days, drenching the roads and creating a sea of mud at the Sodré quay west of Lisbon where a sullen crowd had gathered to watch the embarkation. Prince João was the first to arrive, accompanied by Pedro Carlos (now a young man of twenty-one). They had made the journey in an old carriage with no sign of royal livery and, as João walked across the planks laid over the mud, he heard shouts from the crowd: 'Death to the prince who abandons us!' Distressed by their animosity, as well as by the low-key nature of his departure, he was seen to hold back tears as he boarded the galley which would row him to the flagship (the *Príncipe Real*).

Carlota arrived with her two sons, Pedro and Miguel, her youngest child (a daughter of eleven months) and a wet-nurse, followed by her five elder daughters (aged between two and fourteen). Maria travelled from Queluz in a closed carriage. 'Don't drive so fast!' she cried as the horses galloped towards Lisbon, 'people will think we are fleeing.'[24] When her carriage reached the quayside, she had a fit of hysterics and refused to step down into the mud. 'I don't want to, I don't want to,' she screamed, until a ship's officer picked her up bodily and dropped her into the galley.

The last carriage brought Maria's two sisters, Mariana and Benedita, and after they were safely on board, the servants brought the luggage. More than seven hundred vehicles transported the trunks and treasure chests to the waterside. Most of the contents of the royal palaces were on their way to Brazil: furniture, paintings, gold and silver, vast quantities of diamonds and precious stones, the contents of several libraries, and all the state papers.

There was great confusion on the quays as members of the court and the government, together with large numbers of officials, priests and friars, arrived in carriages, bringing their most valuable pieces of furniture as well as chests packed with their belongings. As soon as it became known that the royal family were sailing for Brazil, the people of Lisbon gathered on the river banks, hoping to find a place on the fifteen warships and thirty merchant vessels anchored in the Tagus. 'Thousands of men, women and children were incessantly on the beach,' wrote an English naval officer, 'endeavouring to effect their escape.'[25]

By evening, the embarkation was complete. More than ten thousand people were on board the Portuguese fleet but a strong wind was blowing from the south-west, trapping the ships in the harbour. They lay at anchor all the following day, while the invasion force was marching closer by the hour. João paced the deck in fear and frustration until, in the early hours of 29 November, the wind shifted to the north-east.

At seven o'clock that morning, the ships moved down the river to join the English squadron waiting outside the bar. As the flagship emerged into open waters, it was greeted by a twenty-one-gun salute from the English fleet, a fearful sound to Maria who had become terrified of loud noises (associating them, perhaps, with the terrors of hell). The return salvo from the *Príncipe Real* was even more terrifying as it reverberated through the hull.

Storm clouds began to gather overhead during the afternoon. The wind veered to the west, the sea took on a heavy swell, and by the time it grew dark, the winds were at gale force. All night and through most of the following day, the ships tacked into the wind, the waves dousing the decks with water.

Over fifteen hundred people were on board the *Príncipe Real* – including Maria, Prince João and his two sons – with insufficient food and water. The royal passengers were relatively comfortable in the staterooms but most of the refugees had to sleep on deck, 'without a bed or any covering, the ladies being destitute of any apparel but what they wore'.[26]

The hull leaked, the rigging was ancient, many of the timbers were rotten, and the ship creaked and groaned as it rode the waves. It took two months to cross the Atlantic to Brazil, eight distressing weeks for Maria who was unaware of the reason for this dramatic flight across the ocean, this sudden plunge into discomfort. 'Where are you taking me?' she kept asking her son. 'What am I doing here?'

18

Exile

The queen's person was in Rio but her imagination presented Lisbonian scenes.
John Luccock, 1820

The ships dropped anchor in the bay of Salvador de Bahia (several hundred miles north of their destination) on 22 January. Prince João and his family disembarked the following morning to find the streets lined with welcoming crowds who were taken aback by the tattered condition of their royal masters. João took his mother and elder son to stay in the governor's palace; the rest of his family remained on board for five days before they took up residence in the law court.

The convoy set sail again on 26 February, following the coastline south to Rio de Janeiro. The ships had been provisioned in Salvador, the weather was calm, and this second leg of the voyage proved that Dr Willis was right about the calming effects of a sea voyage. Maria became calm and pliable, but her demons returned on arrival in Rio. The *Príncipe Real* sailed into the harbour during the afternoon of 7 March to the sound of cannons firing, 'booming salutes that could be heard for miles around'.[27] Maria heard the thunderous sounds in her stateroom and trembled in fear.

After the *Príncipe Real* had dropped anchor, the viceroy came on board to welcome Prince João to the city. He had known for some time that the royal family might arrive for an extended stay. Workmen had converted his residence in the Largo do Paço into a palace for the royal accommodation, monks in an adjacent Carmelite convent had been re-housed and the convent linked to the palace by a covered walkway. The newly-named *Paço Real* had been scrubbed and painted, the state rooms lined in silk. Churches had been cleaned, streets swept, and preparations made for the welcoming ceremonies.

That night, João stood on deck, watching the illuminations in the city and firework displays on the waterfront which crackled and banged into the sky. Next day, he disembarked with his family, leaving Maria on board the flagship. To the sound of gunfire and the pealing of church bells, a brigantine ferried them to the quayside at the Largo do Paço where they were greeted by the viceroy and large numbers of priests and city dignitaries. After kneeling to pray at a temporary altar, they were taken to the palace, their arrival greeted by a twenty-one-gun salute from the artillery drawn up on parade. It was the beginning of a nine-day celebration.

It was planned that Maria should disembark on 9 March and preparations were made to receive her with the same pomp and ceremony which her family had received the previous afternoon. The quayside was lined with aristocrats and priests, the army and militia were drawn up on parade, and Prince João sailed out to the *Príncipe Real* to escort his mother to her new home. But Maria, agitated by the salvos, threw a violent fit when she saw her son, so the landing was postponed until the following day when the welcoming party gathered once again at the waterside.

At five o'clock in the afternoon, as João helped a trembling, black-clad figure into the brigantine, cannons were fired from the forts and from every ship in the harbour. Maria was seen to flinch in fear and, when the guns fired again as the brigantine reached the quay, she shrieked and covered her face with her hands. This demented and terrified old woman was greeted under a silk canopy, bundled into a sedan chair, and carried in procession across the square, 'surrounded by cheers from her vassals, peals of church bells and the cacophonous noise of hundreds of fireworks set off into the air'.

Large crowds had gathered in front of the palace to welcome their sovereign and they cheered as Maria was extracted from the sedan chair and hustled into the palace. She was led along the covered walkway to rooms on the first floor of the Carmelite convent, followed by her family, her ladies-in-waiting and her servants, all of whom queued up to kiss her hand. That evening, João and his family appeared at the palace windows to an eruption of noise from a military parade drawn up in the square:

> There was a twenty-one-gun salute from the artillery, followed by a volley of muskets from the whole infantry, with lots of cheering and applause from the troops and the crowd. This was followed by a second salvo and volley of muskets and more cheering. Then came the third salvo, with a third volley and the same applause.[28]

Maria cowered behind the closed windows of her bedroom. 'Make it stop! Make it stop!' she cried, until one of her attendants passed a message to Prince João. Nine salvos had been scheduled, nine twenty-one-gun salutes outside Maria's windows, but João stopped the proceedings while the guns were being loaded for the fourth salvo, 'in order not to trouble Her Majesty with so much continuous noise'.

The people of Rio could not be silenced so easily. The celebrations in the square continued for the next six days.

The new *Paço Real* lay on the southern side of the Largo do Paço, a square open to the waterfront. The ground floor had been converted into guardrooms and offices, the first floor into accommodation for older members of the family, the attics into bedrooms for the royal children. Adjacent to the palace, on the western side of the square, the two-storey convent building provided the chapel as well as accommodation for Maria and her attendants. Fourteen members of the royal family, together with three hundred servants and attendants, were crammed into these two buildings and into a few single-storey structures at the northern end of the square.

Rio was a noisy, smelly city. Household waste drained away in open channels down the streets and lay in stagnant pools in the low-lying areas, and it was not long before João and Carlota found alternative accommodation in the countryside. João and his sons set up home at Boa Vista, a country estate on a wooded ridge three miles west of the city. Carlota and her daughters moved into a beach house at Botafogo, a quiet inlet inside the bay.

Maria's sisters, Benedita and Mariana, shared the house in Botafogo, leaving the queen alone in the Largo do Paço with her servants and attendants. João came to visit his mother several times a week, but she rarely spoke as he knelt before her and kissed her hand. Carlota and her children also made duty visits. Maria never forgot her position in life ('I am always the queen of Portugal') but other memories surfaced only occasionally. 'This child will wear my crown,' she said one day as she stroked the hair of Pedro, her elder grandson. And she turned to Pedro Carlos, her grandson born in Spain. 'You poor boy!' she said. 'You have no mother, no father.'[29]

It was said that Maria perceived herself to be in Lisbon. If so, she ignored her senses. Her windows overlooked the Largo do Paço, the square filled with people of every different hue. Beyond lay the waterside, the harbour filled with shipping, the great bay edged with high granite mountains. The vegetation was tropical, the heat greater than in Lisbon. The seasons were different too. She was accustomed to the winter rains in Portugal but the rainy season in Rio, which started in September with terrific thunderstorms, was unlike anything she had experienced before. 'There is thunder like I never heard in my life,' wrote a courtier, 'and lightning strikes constantly in the mountains which surround the city.'[30]

Every day in good weather, Maria was taken on outings through the streets of Rio or into the surrounding countryside. Accompanied by a female attendant, she travelled in 'a small chaise drawn by two very ordinary mules and driven by a servant in old and discoloured, if not tattered livery'. A guard accompanied them, 'two soldiers in advance, and twelve following, a single trumpeter and a footman'.[31] There were few horses and mules in Rio, no stables attached to the palace, so Maria's escort was a shabby sight. The guard prepared the way as her chaise moved through the streets and ensured that royal etiquette was obeyed. People had to dismount from their horses, alight from their carriages, and kneel on the ground with bowed heads as the royal chaise passed by.

As the days spread into weeks, the weeks into months, and the months into years, Maria continued to endure her living hell. Sometimes, she would be in a state of lethargy and torpor, impossible to rouse. At other times, she would erupt into violent frenzy, fits of hysteria which could last for days and keep her attendants awake for several nights in succession. She had a high turnover of servants, some of whom mimicked her cries of distress – 'the devil has gotten into me' – and many used the pretext of illness to retire from her service. She would slap and punch them when she was agitated, she would throw plates and scream abuse.

Carlota continued to behave badly, 'displaying great pride and imperiousness, unable to forgive the slightest disrespect', and Benedita settled into old age, becoming 'of mild and sedate habits'.[32] Maria's two grandsons, Pedro and Miguel, grew into reckless young men of little education. Pedro enjoyed mixing with rough company; he toured Rio's taverns in disguise and became notorious for his affairs with women. Miguel (his mother's favourite) took up bullfighting and deer hunting and drove his six-horse carriage at full gallop through the streets.

Every year, the court celebrated Maria's birthday according to protocol. At eleven in the morning, troops marched past the palace windows with the usual discharges of artillery, three salvos from the cannons accompanied by soldiers firing muskets. And while Maria trembled behind the closed windows of her apartment, Prince João conducted a *beija-mão* as foreign diplomats, members of the court, and city dignitaries complimented him on his mother achieving another year of her age.

Discharges of artillery were not confined to birthdays. In May 1810, Maria's Spanish grandson, Pedro Carlos, married his cousin Teresa (João's eldest daughter), the festivities lasting for seven days. In November the following year, there were equally noisy celebrations for the birth of their son Sebastião, Maria's first great-grandchild.

There were deaths too. The first to die, just two years after his marriage, was Pedro Carlos. Several reasons were given for his demise, ranging from smallpox, through 'a violent nervous fever', to – this from the palace gossips – 'excessive conjugal activity'. The following year, it was the turn of Maria's sister, Mariana, who died in May 1813, her body laid to rest in the convent of Nossa Senhora da Ajuda.

Maria herself was next in line. Her robust physical health kept her alive until the advanced age of eighty-one, by which time she had been insane for almost a quarter of a century. Her final illness was painful. She suffered from dysentery and fever, from oedema in her hands and feet, and eventually lost all feeling in her legs. 'There have been moments of relief,' wrote a court official, 'but, once over, the symptoms return stronger than ever.'[33] The doctors tried to alleviate her suffering. Every day, she was taken around the palace in a wheelchair, an ancient figure wracked with inner demons as well as physical pain.

She was confined to bed for the last two months of her life, screaming that she wanted to see nobody, that she wanted to be left alone. But according to protocol, a queen must die surrounded by attendants, ladies-in-waiting, doctors and family, and João remained in thrall to royal etiquette. Every day, as he knelt by the bed to kiss her hand, she screamed at him, 'I don't want to see anyone! I want to die!'[34]

Maria received the last rights on 19 March 1816, on a warm autumn evening as crowds gathered in the square beneath her windows. Early the following morning, João came to kiss her hand for the last time. She died a few hours later and, as soon as the news was announced, bells began to toll and twenty-one-gun salutes were fired every ten minutes until midnight. At last Maria was safe from the sounds which had terrified her for so long.

Her attendants dressed her in a black gown covered with a red velvet cloak. They laid a cloth of gold damask over her body, leaving her right arm exposed. A crucifix hung on the wall above the bed and four silver candelabras were placed around the body. The following day, there was a final *beija-mão* as Maria's family, the nobility, the priests and city dignitaries, all came to kiss her right hand, to pray for her soul and sprinkle her body with holy water.

The ritual lasted all day. Vast numbers of people filed through the room to pay their final respects to a queen whom most of them had known only as *Maria A Louca*, Maria the Mad.

19

Return to Portugal

It is a great hardship for us little people that a queen cannot be interred without rendering many of her subjects distracted.
Marianne Baillie, 8 April 1822

To protect his mother's modesty, João gave orders that her body should not be embalmed. Instead, she was placed in an inner coffin lined with llama wool. This was inserted into a second coffin made of lead and, before the lids were sealed, the spaces in both coffins were filled with aromatic gums, spices and dried herbs. The lead coffin was then placed inside a third coffin of polished wood, with a cross of gold damask on the lid. This outer coffin was fastened with two locks and the keys placed in the care of the Marquis de Angeja (grandson of Maria's first secretary of state).

The following evening, the coffin was carried down the stairs to the main doors of the palace where the royal coach was waiting. The streets were lined with soldiers, crowded with people who fell silent as the royal cortège passed by. The queen's arrival at the convent of Nossa Senhora da Ajuda was greeted by a twenty-one-gun salute from the battalions drawn up by the door. A requiem mass was performed in the chapel, after which Maria was carried into the mausoleum to be interred alongside the body of her sister.

João was confined to the palace during the funeral formalities which lasted for eight days. On 28 March, he held an official audience to mark his return to public life; the following day, he visited the convent at Ajuda. His mother had been insane since 1792 but he found it difficult to let her go. He declared court mourning for a full year and the anniversaries of her death (the week, the month, the year) were marked by solemn ceremonies.

The people of Rio were expecting the acclamation of their new king, João VI, to take place a few weeks later. But João deferred the ceremony for almost two years, partly because of the marriage of his elder son in 1817 (to a Hapsburg princess), partly because of a revolutionary uprising in the province of Pernambuco, but mainly because he was concerned about his mother's immortal soul, the truth of her salvation.

João had lived for more than two decades with his mother's conviction that she was destined for hellfire. He asked the priests for confirmation that she had passed from the state of purgatory, 'but on this the wise men differed. The priests of the royal chapel declared that she had entered upon perfect bliss, while those of Nossa Senhora de Candelária maintained that she was not yet purified.'[35]

On the far side of the Atlantic, the Peninsular War had taken its toll on the people whom Prince João had abandoned to their fate. When peace was declared in 1814, it was assumed that he would sail home to reinvigorate a country exhausted and disorganised after eight years of war. A British squadron was sent to escort the royal family to Lisbon but, happy in Rio and dreading the thought of another sea voyage, João decided to remain in Brazil.

He was only persuaded to return home after a revolution in Portugal brought a constitutional government to power in November 1820. The world Maria knew – a world of absolute monarchy, clerical dominance of affairs of state, and ancient court protocol – had been swept away by the upheavals of the French Revolution and the Napoleonic Wars. João had been isolated from events in Europe. He hated the very idea of a constitution but in February 1821, when riots broke out in Rio, he agreed to return to Portugal and accept the new political reality. He would leave his elder son, Pedro, to act as regent in Brazil.

Before dawn on the morning of 25 April, the royal family (João, his aunt Benedita, his wife Carlota, his younger son

Miguel and four of his daughters) embarked on the *Dom João VI*, the new flagship of the Portuguese fleet. The bodies of Maria and her sister Mariana were travelling with them. Their coffins had been disinterred and carried on board, Maria's coffin placed in solitary state in a cabin fitted out as a chapel. She would lie here for ten weeks as the flagship took her home across the ocean.

Next morning, thirteen ships set sail for Lisbon. When they arrived in the Tagus on 3 July, the harbour was filled with boats, the river banks lined with people eager to catch a glimpse of a royal family which had been absent for almost fourteen years. After three invasions of their country, with appalling destruction and loss of life, the king and his family appeared like relics from another age.

João stood on deck wearing a plumed hat, his pronounced stomach emphasised by a gold-embroidered uniform studded with medals and orders. Carlota (well under five feet tall) was seen in animated conversation, her younger son Miguel at her side. Benedita wore a black dress embroidered with diamonds and appeared – in the words of the French ambassador – 'just like an old picture that has stepped out of its frame'.[36]

The family went ashore the following day and João was taken to parliament where, 'with a wild and distrustful expression', he swore to uphold the constitution. Having loathed each other for decades, he and Carlota set up separate establishments, João in the convent of Bemposta where he did his best to act fairly to the new regime, Carlota in the palace of Queluz where she lived with Miguel, plotting the downfall of the constitution. An absolutist in every fibre of her being, she instilled in her son a deep conviction in the divine right of kings.

João, meanwhile, had decided to break with custom. Maria would not join her husband, elder son and three infant children in the royal mausoleum at São Vicente de Fora. Instead she would lie in the Basilica da Estrela, the church she had built in thanksgiving for the birth of Prince José, the church she had dedicated to the Heart of Jesus. For the next nine months, as her coffin was moved from one convent to another, a tomb of black and white marble was built in the right transept of the basilica, close to that of Inácio de São Caetano – the confessor who took her soul upon himself – which stands across the nave in the sacristy.

Maria was given a state funeral in March 1822. The ceremonies, accompanied by cannon-fire and the continuous tolling of bells, lasted for three days and nights. 'The great guns on sea and land and the bells of every steeple in Lisbon,' wrote an Englishwoman who found it impossible to sleep through the noise, 'thundered and pealed without intermission. It is a great hardship for us little people that a queen cannot be interred without rendering many of her subjects distracted. I am sure many sick persons must have been hurried out of the world by the sheer noise.'[37]

As the coffin was brought to Estrela, the royal family drove by in carriages, followed by the aristocracy on horseback wearing black coats and hats with long black streamers. Then came the religious establishment, a long procession of bishops, priests and friars, and the army, regiment after regiment, their bands playing funeral music. The Marquis de Angeja delivered the keys he had been given in Rio and which he had guarded safely for more than six years. The locks of the outer coffin were opened, the lead coffin was cut open, the lid of the inner coffin unscrewed.

Two of Maria's grand-daughters presided over the ceremony of dressing the corpse in new clothes, a duty performed by their unfortunate ladies-in-waiting. The body had not been embalmed. It had spent five years in a tropical climate and, despite the herbs and spices, the stench was overpowering. One of the princesses fainted twice and refused to return to the proceedings.

The dead queen was dressed in a black robe, with cap, gloves, shoes and stockings. She lay exposed in the church for two days, watched over by a guard of honour, while members of the nobility came to pay their last respects and kiss her freshly-gloved hand. It was said that the corpse was still entire, the limbs still flexible, although the face had turned a deep shade of black.

Above Maria's tomb rests a carved plaque with her portrait in profile, held on one side by an angel blowing a trumpet, on the other by a relaxed and cheerful cherub. João commissioned this image of his mother accompanied by angels, perhaps to reassure himself that her fears were unfounded, that she had earned her place in heaven, that she had indeed 'entered upon perfect bliss'.

Epilogue

1822–1832

Four years later, the death of João VI brings Maria's story to a close. Portugal was in political turmoil after the king's return to Lisbon, with his younger son Miguel – encouraged by his mother – fighting a rearguard action against the constitution. Miguel was, unlike his father (and giving rise to rumours about his paternity), tall, slim and good-looking, and Carlota used him as a figurehead for her schemes to restore the absolute power of monarchy.

João lived in fear of the violence unleashed by Miguel and was troubled to the end of his days by his malign and vengeful wife. His elder son Pedro declared himself emperor of an independent Brazil and, after João's death, he and Miguel began to battle for control of Portugal. Pedro espoused the liberal, constitutional cause; Miguel shared his mother's absolutist principles.

The story that began when Maria welcomed a tiny Spanish princess to Vila Viçosa ended with the outbreak of civil war (the War of the Two Brothers) in 1832, two years after Carlota followed her husband to the grave.

APPENDICES

Account of the royal visit to Marinha Grande

Philadephia Stephens
Marinha Grande, 25 July 1788

On Monday the 30th ult° at four o'clock in the afternoon, Her Majesty and all the Royal Family arrived here accompanied by their *Donas*, *Açafatas*, Confessors, Physician, Secretary of State,[1] *Camaristas*, *Guardaroupas*, Chaplains, Surgeons, *Reposteiros*, *Moças da Prata*, etc., with numberless other people belonging to their Suite. The Royal Family drove straight to the church, where they spent a few minutes in prayers, when they got into their carriages again and came to our house. Our *Praça* on this occasion made a very brilliant appearance. On each side of the house, the soldiers were drawn up in form belonging to the Guard and opposite, before the door of the Fabrick, all the artificers belonging to the manufactory in their working dress which does not admit of either coat or waistcoat, their hair dressed and powdered, their shirts clean and ironed with the sleeves tied round the middle of the arm with red ribbons, black breeches and clean white stockings which altogether gave them a very neat uniform appearance.

On the carriages entering the gate, the Royal Family were saluted with three *Vivas* from the people of the Fabrick and on alighting at the door of the house were received by the Archbishop (the Queen's confessor),[2] my brother William, my brothers Lewis and Jedediah, the Visconde de Ponte de Lima,[3] and *Camaristas*. Your humble servant had the honour of kissing Her Majesty's hand on her entrance and received a gracious smile in return. The same ceremony was repeated

1 Viscount de Ponte de Lima
2 Inácio de São Caetano, Archbishop of Thessalonica
3 Secretary of state for home affairs and acting first minister

with the Princess[4] and each of the Infantas.[5] On the arrival of the *Donas* and *Açafatas*, the Archbishop introduced me to them and recommended them to my particular care. Madame Arriaga is a very clever, agreeable, well-bred lady.[6] She is a widow and a great favourite of the Queen's. I describe her in particular supposing you have often heard her name mentioned.

The Royal Family immediately went upstairs and, after viewing their own apartment on the principal floor, Her Majesty went up to the attic story to see the accommodations of her female attendants with which she expressed great satisfaction. When she had done looking at the apartments, she intimated a desire of seeing the Fabrick. Accordingly a procession of the Royal Family and attendants walked across the *Praça* from the house to the Fabrick amidst a vast concourse of people. On their entrance into the Fabrick, they were again saluted by the manufacturers with '*Viva a Rainha, Viva toda a Familia Real*' repeated three times. The Royal Family took their seats in a *varanta* prepared for the purpose covered with green baize and crimson taffety where they spent about half an hour amusing themselves with seeing the people at work. The Princess, afraid of being so near the glass furnace on account of the heat so soon after finishing her baths at the Caldas, immediately on entering the Fabrick called me to her and desired I would shew her the way upstairs to the packing warehouse. Accordingly I ordered a chair to be placed for her by the window where she amused herself in admiring the prospect and talking to me and to D. José Lobo, her *Camarista*, in a very agreeable familiar style during the time the Queen remained down in the *varanta*. Her Majesty, after satisfying her curiosity of seeing the people at work and applauding them all very much, came upstairs and examined everything very attentively.

After spending a little time here, they took a view of the other departments belonging to the Fabrick. In the cutting and flowering room,[7] they sat some time admiring the work, the Queen and Princess both asking me a number of questions about our craftsmen etc. After taking a view of everything belonging to the Fabrick, they walked into

4 Benedita, Princess of Brazil, sister of Maria I and wife to Prince José
5 Mariana (sister of Maria I) and Carlota Joaquina (wife of Prince João)
6 Madame Arriaga, a senior *açafata* and Maria's favourite female attendant
7 The workshop where glass was cut, engraved and painted with flowers

the garden where chairs were placed in different situations for them to rest themselves. Here they diverted themselves till Ave Marias, when they retired to the house and drank tea.

Immediately on finishing tea, they went to the theatre where the gallery was elegantly prepared for their reception, the whole being hung round with crimson damask and the front ornamented with crimson damask curtains trimmed with gold lace and hung in festoons, the rails covered with crimson velvet ornamented with a deep gold fringe. On the right hand of the Royal Gallery was a side gallery for the Archbishop and, opposite on the left hand side, a similar gallery for the *Donas* and *Açafatas*, behind which was sufficient room for all the rest of the female attendants to see the play. The pit was allotted for such people belonging to the suite as were not *Camaristas* or in immediate waiting, as also for the gentlemen of this neighbourhood and the *Ministros* of the City of Leiria. There was also a private box under the Royal Gallery for the principal ladies of Leiria who were here to see the entertainments.

Immediately on Her Majesty's entrance in the gallery, the orchestra, which consisted of four violins, two French horns and two violoncellos, began the overture, during the performance of which the Royal Family admired the design and painting of the curtain. It represents a lady sitting upon a large tree with the Arms of Portugal by her side and a youth in a light gardener's dress emptying a cornucopia in her lap as the emblem of Plenty and Industry. The expulsion of Indolence is represented by a beggar who is a healthy, stout, hearty-looking fellow covered with rags, his pockets stuffed with bread, and a staff in his hand pointed with iron serves as an offensive or defensive weapon as best suits his purpose. He is going off with a look of contempt on Industry. The explanation at the bottom is in the following words: '*Lusitania pelas Artes recebe da Industria Abundancia e desterra a Mendicidade*'.[8] Over the front of the stage, two female figures representing Tragedy and Comedy are supporting a target with the following label, '*Vinde e descansai porque trabalhistas*',[9] alluding to the motives for which the theatre was built.

8 'Portugal receives Abundance from Industry and Indigence is exiled'
9 'Come and rest from your labours'

On finishing the overture, the curtain was drawn up and the Tragedy of *Sésostris* commenced.[10] This play was by particular desire of Her Majesty and I must do our young people the justice to say that, although they had not a fortnight to study it, they performed their parts exceedingly well. Between the acts, there were different dances and pantomimes, during which the Royal Family were served with ice of different sorts[11] and other refreshments. After the play, the farce of *Esganarello* was performed with great applause.

As soon as the theatrical amusements finished, the Royal Family returned to the house where they found supper on the table and the *Praça* illuminated with about two thousand lights, disposed on frames hung in the following manner [diagram], which covered all the walls of the buildings between the windows, an obelisk in the middle of the *Praça* crowned with a sphere at the top. Two triumphal cars with musick were drawn round the square and played under the windows during the time of supper and, as soon as the Royal Family got up from table, some pretty fireworks were displayed off which amused them about a quarter of an hour, when they all retired to their apartments and a total silence commenced for the night.

The Royal Family supped together in our large room at a table twenty-two *palmos* long and eleven wide. The Queen sat in the centre on one side of the table, with the Princess on her right hand side and the Infanta Dona Carlota on the left, the Infanta Dona Mariana at the left hand of Dona Carlota. On the opposite side of the table fronting the Princess sat the Prince[12] with his brother Dom João at his right hand opposite Dona Carlota. Their usual custom at Lisbon and the Caldas is to sup and dine each in their different apartments; in travelling they in general eat together and, on this occasion, they seemed to be very happy in each other's company.

The table and sideboards were hung round with pink-coloured *nobreza*; in the centre of the large table was a very elegant glass ornament made here, representing a temple. The design was given by the Marquis of Marialva's *Copeiro* who had the direction of all the confectionery with the assistance of the Queen's Confectioner who

10 *Sésostris* (1695) by Hilaire Bernard de Longpierre (translated into Portuguese in 1785)

11 Ice creams and sorbets

12 José, Prince of Brazil, elder son of Maria I

undertook mostly the management of the ice, of which there was a great variety and exceeding good. The custom is to put everything on the table at once, meat, fruit, sweetmeats etc. All the dishes from the kitchen is served up by the direction of Her Majesty's Chief Cook, who had three and twenty cooks to work under him.

When the Royal Family arose from table, the *Donas* and *Açafatas* and your humble servant sat down. It is the usual custom in journeys for the *Camaristas* and Noblemen to sit down at the table after the Royal Family. It is then called *Mesa de Estado*, but on this occasion it was judged most expedient for the ladies to remain upstairs and the *Mesa de Estado* for the *Camaristas* and Secretary of state was placed in our dining room on the ground floor. This table was a little smaller than the Royal one. It had a pyramid of glass salvers in the middle decorated with sweetmeats and the table hung round with blue *nobreza*. The Archbishop had a separate table in his apartment for himself and companion Padre Rocha, the late Provincial of the Order of St. Domingos,[13] as had also some others belonging to different departments.

At the upper end of our great walk in the garden was erected a wooden *barraca*, eighty *palmos* long and thirty wide, hung with tapestry and covered with sailcloth. In this room was a table containing about fifty or sixty people, where my brother entertained the *Cavalheiros da Província*, Ministers and Câmara de Leiria and all such company as could not be admitted at the other tables.

The Royal Family and their female attendants were all lodged in our house which, on this occasion, was called the *Paço* or Palace, the Archbishop in the house on the right hand side of the gate, and the *Camaristas* and Secretary of state etc. at the best house in the place, where we had very excellent beds made for them. The livery servants, coachmen and soldiers with their beasts were all well accommodated under the wood sheds, where they had their kitchen and dining rooms according to their several degrees, with a plentiful supply of the best beef, rice and bread that could be got in this country and as much *Aljubarrota* wine as they chose to drink. Notwithstanding this, for their honour, I must not omit saying that there was not one got drunk,

13 Father Rocha, Dominican friar, confessor and companion to Inácio de São Caetano

nor the least disturbance happened during the whole time they were here, and as a remarkable proof of their honesty, I can assure you that on this, and the former occasion of their being here, we lost nothing but two dessert spoons which I suppose to be mislaid or thrown out with the dirt of the kitchen, it being not an object to be stolen where there was an opportunity of stealing things of a much greater value.

You may guess a little more or less of the number of people belonging to Her Majesty's suite when I tell you that we had stables provided with straw and barley for six hundred beasts exclusive of the troops. Besides the people belonging to the Court, there was a vast concourse from all the country round this neighbourhood which curiosity had brought together to see their Sovereign, with whom they seemed mightily pleased.

On Tuesday morning, the first inst., the Infante Dom João got up at four o'clock and took a ride with a few attendants to see his estates at Monte Real, the camp of Leiria, and the works at the Foz da Vieira two leagues distant.[14] He examined the whole very minutely and returned very well pleased with his excursion between eight and nine o'clock. By this time, the Queen and all the Royal Family were up and dressed. They breakfasted in their different apartments on tea and *tosta Inglesa*. Breakfast being over, their travelling altar was erected in the Queen's dressing room, where Mass was celebrated by one of Her Majesty's Chaplains in the presence of the Royal Family and a few of their attendants. This being over, they amused themselves in walking about the house and conversing very affable with any persons who came in their way.

Between one and two o'clock, dinner was served up in the same manner as the preceding supper. During coffee, the carriages were got ready, when they took a ride with a few attendants to see the famous and ancient city of Leiria. After passing under a Triumphant Arch erected by the Câmara or Chamber at the entrance of the city, they drove straight to the Cathedral Church where they were received with the usual ceremonies by the Bishop. On their first going to any church, it is the custom for the Bishop or the Principal Priest belonging to the church to receive the Queen at the door under the canopy which they

---

14 Foz da Vieira, mouth of the River Liz, where engineers were removing sandbanks which narrowed the entrance channel

carry over the Sacrament. In this manner, she walks with the Royal Family up to the High Altar where velvet cushions are placed for them to kneel on. During their private prayers, a short Te Deum is sung, accompanied by such musick as the church affords. This being finished, they retire in the same manner they entered.

After viewing the cathedral, they went in their carriage to the Bishop's Palace, which is very spacious and well furnished. It is situated on an eminence and commands a most beautiful prospect of the city. The ruins of an old Moorish castle, the river and the country adjacent, they saw the whole with great pleasure and, after partaking of an elegant *merenda*, they left the palace and went to the Convent of nuns of the Dominican order. After seeing the church, they went into the Convent and examined every corner of it with satisfaction. They left the poor nuns highly impressed with gratitude, not only for the honour of the visit, but also for Her Majesty's gracious bounty of twenty *Moydores* which she left for their support. Thirty *Moydores* were also ordered to be given to the poor of the city. At the Convent door, they got into their carriages vastly delighted with the City of Leiria which, on this occasion, made a great figure, the houses being all whitewashed, the streets covered with sand, and the windows hung with curtains the same as on grand procession days. At Ave Marias, they all arrived here again safe.

The Prince and his brother left Leiria some time before the Queen. They came part of the road in a chaise, then mounted their horses and took a ride to see the Timber Fabrick and the Forest,[15] which is near our house, but arrived here at the same time with the Queen. After drinking tea, they went again to the theatre with the same ceremonies as the preceding night and saw the comedy of *Dom José de Alvarado, Criado de Sigmesmo*.[16] It's a laughable piece and was acted with great humour. At the end of the second act, a solo was played on the violoncello by a young man of Leiria who is studying physic at Coimbra, as a *curioso*. He plays very well and the Royal Family applauded much his performance. Between the other acts were different dances and pantomimes, the whole concluded with the farce of the *Letrado Avarento*.[17]

---

15 The state-owned sawmill and royal pine forest of Leiria

16 *Dom José de Alvarado, Servant of Himself*

17 *The Miserly Scholar*

The theatre was illuminated with wax and the dresses on each night new according to the characters. The performers acquitted themselves with honour and received universal applause, not only from the Royal Family but from all the audience who thought it impossible that a rude country place like this could have produced such good actors. Their surprise was greatly increased on finding that the greatest part of them had never been more than two or three leagues from this parish, and that they all worked in the Fabrick. They perform only for their amusement, which you must allow is very different from the public theatres where the actors have no other employment than studying their parts and their whole subsistence depends upon the favourable opinion of the public.

The amusements of the theatre being finished, the Royal Family returned to the house where supper, illuminations, triumphal cars and fireworks concluded the diversions in the same manner as on the preceding night.

The next morning, Wednesday the 2nd inst., the Royal Family arose early, dressed, breakfasted and heard Mass in the same manner as before mentioned, during which everything was got ready for their departure between eight and nine o'clock. The Prince and Princess[18] got into their carriage and drove straight through to the Caldas, being afraid to stop and dine at Nazaré on account of the smallpox which raged there, it being doubtful whether the Prince had [had] this disorder or not. On taking leave of Her Royal Highness, I kissed her hand and thanked her for the honour she had done us in this visit and wished her a good journey. In return she gave me an *abraço*, thanked me for the hospitable entertainments she had received, and wished me health and happiness. My brother took leave of the Prince in the same manner and attended him to the door of the carriage.

On driving out of the gate, they were again saluted with three *Vivas*. Her Majesty and the rest of the Royal Family remained near an hour after the Prince and Princess were gone. On the Queen's leaving her apartment, I kissed her hand when she thanked me for the entertainment we had given her, with a countenance that indicated she was pleased with everything she had seen. I then took leave of the Infantas Dona Mariana and Dona Carlota. The former gave me an

18 José and Benedita, Prince and Princess of Brazil

abraço and repeated her thanks in the same manner as the Queen and Princess.

At the bottom of the stairs, the Administrator of the Fabrick, with the two Book-keepers and Paymaster, were introduced and kissed Her Majesty's hand who received them very graciously and applauded very much the industry of our people, the good order and management of the Fabrick, and the harmony which subsisted between the people belonging to the Manufactory. They then went through the ceremony with the Infante Dom João and the two Infantas, who also received them very graciously. In the hall were the Bishop of Leiria with his attendants and the *Ministros* and *Câmara* of Leiria who took leave in the same manner.

My brother attended Her Majesty to the door of the carriage where she again repeated her thanks for his hospitality and drove away amidst the acclamations of a great number of people who remained penetrated with love and respect for their Sovereign and all the Royal Family for their pleasing and affable deportment during their stay in this place. From our house they went to the church. After a few minutes in prayer there, they went to the borders of the Forest and, from thence, to Nazaré where they paid their usual devotions to *Nossa Senhora*,[19] dined, went to the *praia* to see some nets drawn with fish, and from thence to the Caldas where they slept that night and rested the next day, Thursday.

On Friday the 4th inst., they returned to Lisbon where they speak with high encomiums of the entertainment they received here. In short, my brother has attained what nobody else in the Kingdom can boast of, which is the honour of entertaining the Royal Family and all the Court for two days, and given universal satisfaction to everybody from the Queen down to the scullions and stable boys. The first time of Her Majesty's coming here was not so surprising, as curiosity to see the Glass Fabrick was supposed to be the motive, but that she should come a second time and sleep two nights in the house of a private person, an Englishman and a Protestant, is a thing that never entered the idea of the Portuguese and has struck all those country people with amazement. Her Majesty liked her situation so well that she regretted leaving it and would have stayed longer had it not been for the

19 Nossa Senhora de Nazaré, Chapel of Our Lady of Nazaré

unavoidable necessity of returning so soon to Lisbon. The orders were already passed for the change of beasts on the road and everything to be got ready for their reception at the Praça de Comércio[20] and it was now too late to recede. She left one hundred *Moydores* to be distributed among the people of the Fabrick and twenty *Moydores* for the poor of the parish.

Immediately on Her Majesty's leaving us, our house was open for every person who chose to see it. We had a large company from Leiria and the neighbourhood who dined with us at the Royal Table and, at night, the same illuminations were repeated. The Tragedy of *Sésostris*, with the same new dresses, dances and pantomimes as on the first night, were performed with universal applause to a numerous audience, free admittance being granted (as is our usual custom to every person of all ranks and denominations). After the play, our company supped with us at the Royal Table, drank Her Majesty's health, and concluded our three days festival with no small satisfaction to ourselves and all our neighbours, it being altogether such a sight as they had never seen before.

A few days previous to Her Majesty's arrival here, the Chief Director of the Household came with the *Armador* who brought five beds for the Royal Family and curtains for the doors and windows of the principal rooms. They were of crimson damask trimmed with gold lace and valance of crimson velvet with a deep gold fringe. The Prince and Princess's bed was very large and elegant. The stands were iron gilt, the boards painted white. Over them was a crimson buckram covering with crimson damask valance fastened to it. The headboard was covered with crimson damask, over which was a case of a most beautiful fine muslin worked with small spots of silver, the edges trimmed with an elegant silver blond lace plaited on pretty thick. The first mattress was of a very fine new *pano de linho* which they brought empty and filled here with rye straw. Over this was two mattresses of very fine Irish linen stuffed with wool. These were covered with a very good *pano de linho* sheet which four men pulled with all their strength and tucked in under the straw mattress. Next was a fine Irish linen sheet tucked in in the same manner. Two flat bolsters were then laid on each other, stuffed with wool and quilted in the same manner as the mattresses. The bolster cases were plain but of finer linen than the

20 A reception to welcome the Queen when her barge returned to the city

sheets. The upper sheet of fine Irish linen was then put on with a crimson damask coverlid, the part of the sheet which turns down being tucked to the coverlid. Over this, instead of a blanket, was an orange-colour broadcloth covering bound with ribbon of the same colour. This covering was to be taken off, or put on, at pleasure. Upon this was another crimson damask coverlid which was also tucked in very tight under the straw mattress and the whole was covered with the same elegant silver-spotted muslin as the headboard, with a deep full flounce that reached from the upper mattress to the floor, the whole trimmed with silver blond lace. The state round bolster was then laid on the bed in a case of the same muslin trimmed in the same manner as the coverlid and the ends tied with large knots of the best English white ribbon. A crimson taffety covering was then thrown lightly over the whole to keep off the dust.

The Queen's bedstead was the same as the Princess's but smaller and the mattresses, flat bolsters and sheets the same as has been already described. Instead of an orange-colour broadcloth covering, hers was white, the headboard was covered with crimson damask, the same as the coverlid and valance, without any other ornament than being bound with silk lace of the same colour.

The Infantas Dona Mariana, Dona Carlota and the Infante Dom João's bedsteads were all three of brazilwood, the mattresses, bolsters and covering the same as the Queen's, except the Infanta Dona Carlota, whose bed was made in the English style. The sheets which she brought from Spain were remarkably fine but plain, the bolster was round with a cambric case bordered at each end with a fine flowered muslin. The coverlid was white satin quilted *à Inglesa*, over which was thrown a crimson taffety covering to preserve it from dust.

The bedstead had posts and mosquito nets. The Queen's and Princess's had testers and curtains belonging to them but Her Majesty, most graciously recollecting that our rooms being elegantly furnished with stucco, the testers could not be fastened without driving hooks into the ceiling, for which reason she gave positive orders for the beds to be made without curtains as she would not consent by any means for the most trifling thing to be done to injure the house which she often admired for its neatness. She very politely took every opportunity of praising everything. After dinner, she told me she had eaten very hearty, everything being exceeding good.

The Marquis de Pombal[21] was the only person who brought his bed, except the five of the Royal Family. All the rest were provided by us, which altogether amounted to some hundreds which we got from Leiria and its neighbourhood, it being impossible to collect so great a number in this place. The livery servants and soldiers were delighted to find they had got decent beds to sleep in. It was a luxury they enjoyed for the first time since leaving Lisbon on the 3rd of May. During the whole time of their being at the Caldas, they were obliged to sleep on loose straw in the stables, on the ground, or wheresoever they could find a place to lay themselves down, such is the hardship these poor fellows endure when travelling with the Court and is probably the reason of their committing many outrages, but I must again repeat that their good behaviour here entitled them to every indulgence.

The Royal Family are waited upon at table by their *Camaristas* and *Reposteiros*. On the Queen's entering the dining room, she is presented by her *Camarista* on his knee with water and a towel to wash her hands, which being done she takes her seat and the *Camarista* stands behind her chair. The same ceremony is observed with all the rest of the Royal Family. The *Camarista* then carves such dishes as they choose to eat of and, when anything is required from the sideboards, the *Reposteiros* reach it to the *Camarista* who puts it on the table. When water or wine is required, the *Reposteiro* draws the cork and brings the bottle and glass on a salver to the *Camarista* who, on his knee, pours out the liquor and presents it to the Queen, remaining in the same attitude to receive the glass when she has done drinking.

When dinner is over, they again wash their hands and retire to drink coffee. They are very particular with respect to the water they drink which is all brought in flasks from Lisbon, some from the Chafariz da Praia[22] and some from the Ajuda. One of the *Reposteiros*, who was *Provedor das Aguas*, I observed had nothing else to do but to keep the key of the water chests and take care that there was always a bottle full of water ready on the sideboard and on a table in each of the apartments. Her Majesty's bottle was distinguished by having a bit of narrow white ribbon tied round the neck. Claret is the wine chiefly made use of, and that only a very small quantity.

---

21 2nd Marquis of Pombal, gentleman of the bedchamber

22 One of the highly-decorated fountains in Lisbon which supplied water to the people

Her Majesty I found greatly improved in her looks since she was here in the year 1786, being now fatter, of a better colour and more cheerful countenance. The Princess is something thinner but still retains a pleasant agreeable aspect. The Infanta Dona Mariana is fatter and, although not handsome, has something agreeable and majestic in her appearance. The Infanta Dona Carlota appears just the same as when she was here last, lively but very short, nor does her countenance indicate that she will ever grow much taller. I have seen children as lusty at nine years of age; she is now in her fourteenth.

The Queen, Princess and Infantas were dressed in silk riding habits, every day a different one. Her Majesty wears her hair twined up before in a plain tight toupee, behind in a bag like the gentlemen or in a queue. She makes use of a little old-fashioned cocked hat which she generally carries in her hand or under her arm. It is seldom she puts it on her head but when she rides on horseback. The Princess had her hair frizzed before and tied in a club behind. She wore a large hat in the English fashion, round the crown of which was a ribbon with a knot on one side ornamented with steel bows. The two Infantas were also nearly in the same style with the Princess. They all wore broad black velvet girdles round the waist, fastened before with two monstrous large medallions, set and ornamented with steel, which I believe were English.

The *Donas* and *Açafatas* are not allowed to wear either riding dresses or hats, let the journey be ever so long and the wind, sun and dust ever so troublesome. They are obliged to travel through it in chaises dressed in the same manner as we English people commonly do on Friday nights when we go to the Long Room.[23] No person is allowed to sit in the presence of any of the Royal Family, except the Archbishop who is the Queen's Confessor. The *Camaristas*, when tired of standing, may rest themselves by kneeling on one knee whilst talking or playing at cards. The *Donas* and *Açafatas* have sometimes leave to sit on the floor.

The expense of this entertainment was about a fifth part of what is computed by people in general, notwithstanding my brother amply rewarded the Cooks and *Copeiros* for their trouble. Previous to their

23 Ballroom of the British Assembly Rooms in Lisbon

coming, everything was provided for them so that, on their arrival, they had nothing to do but begin their work. We required nothing from Her Majesty's Household but the damask hangings for the doors and windows and the large coppers for the use of the kitchen. China, Damask, Table and Plate we have sufficient for the service of all the different tables. Having had some reason to expect this visit last year, we got a large supply of silver-hafted knives and forks and spoons from England, of the best quality and newest fashion, all which is carefully preserved for the next occasion, which probably will be next year as the Royal Family have some thought of going to Coimbra.

A little anecdote happened which is scarcely worth mention only as a proof of Her Majesty's determined resolution to be pleased with everything she met with. The Queen and Princess have each a particular teapot and cup and saucer which they always make use of. The Princess brought hers. The female servant who packed it up enquired of the Queen if she would have hers packed up also, to which Her Majesty said 'No', that she knew very well Stephens had provided everything that was requisite and she was determined to make use of nothing but what belonged to his house.

Glossary

(Portuguese words in italics)

A/O	The
Abraço	Embrace or hug
Açafata	Junior lady-in-waiting. Maria I had several dozen *açafatas* in attendance
Ague	Cold fit with shivering, a symptom of malaria
Aljubarrota	Village near Marinha Grande; wine from this locality
Armador	Royal servant who assembled furniture, hung curtains and oversaw the decorations when the royal family moved from one residence to another
Artificer	Craftsman; workman with skill
Ave Marias	Used to denote time of day
Bacalhau	Dried and salted fish
Bag	Silken pouch to contain hair at the back of the head (18th-century usage)
Barraca	Wooden barrack; marquee
Barraca Real	Royal palace built of wood at Ajuda
Beija-mão	Kissing of hands
Bergantim	Barge
Bergantim Real	Royal barge
Câmara	Chamber; town council
Camarista	Lord of the bedchamber
Cavalheiros	Gentlemen
Cavalheiros da Província	Gentlemen of the province

Chafariz	Fountain
Chaise	Two-wheeled carriage
Club	Club-shaped knot or bun of hair worn at the top or back of the head (fashionable in the late 18th century)
Comércio	Business; commerce
Copeiro	Household official in charge of drinks and confectionery
Cruzado	Coin worth 400 *reis*
Curioso	Curiosity
Dom	Title given to men of royal birth
Dona	Title given to women of royal birth; senior lady-in-waiting of noble birth
Dropsy	Archaic medical term for oedema (fluid retention in bodily tissues)
e	and
Fabrick	Factory
Familia	Family
Foz	Mouth of a river
Guardaroupa	Servant in charge of the royal wardrobe
Infanta	Princess
Infante	Prince
Inglesa	English
à Inglesa	In the English style
Largo	Small square
League	Measurement of distance (one league = three miles)
Louco/Louca	Mad, insane
Merenda	Light meal; collation
Mesa de estado	State table
Milreis	One thousand *reis*
Ministros	Men with official positions in a town or city
Moças da Prata	Female servants in charge of the royal silver

Moydore (moidore)	Coin worth 4000 *reis* (4 *milreis*)
Nobreza	Nobility; rich silk cloth used by the nobility
Nossa Senhora	Our Lady
Paço	Palace
Palmo	Measurement of the long side of the hand (one *palmo* = about eight inches)
Pano de linho	Fine linen cloth
Praça	Square; courtyard
Praia	Beach
Príncipe	Prince
Provedor	Comptroller; superintendent of office
Provedor das aguas	*Reposteiro* in charge of provision of drinking water
Província	Province; neighbourhood
Queue	Long plait of hair hanging down from the back of the head
Quinta	Country house; estate
Rainha	Queen
Reposteiro	Footman
Real	Royal; basic unit of currency
Reis	Currency, plural of *real*
Taffety	Taffeta
Terreiro	Square; place of
Terremoto	Earthquake
Tester	Canopy over a bed
Todo/toda	All
Tosta	Toast
Toupee	Hair at front of the head combed up over a pad into a top-knot (18th-century usage)
Varanta	Veranda; pavilion
Visconde	Viscount
Viva	Long live (used as a cheer)

Cast of Characters

Bragança Family

Bárbara (1711–1758)
Maria's aunt.
Daughter of João V, elder sister to José I. Married Ferdinand de Bourbon (later Ferdinand VI of Spain) in 1729.

Benedita (1746–1829)
Maria's sister and daughter-in-law.
Fourth and youngest daughter of José I. Married her nephew, Crown Prince José, in 1777 (becoming known as the Princess of Brazil). Died in Queluz in 1829.

Carlota Joaquina (de Bourbon, 1775–1830)
Maria's daughter-in-law.
Daughter of Charles IV of Spain. Married Prince João in 1785. Became queen-consort when João inherited the throne in 1816. Died in Lisbon in 1830.

Doroteia (1739–1771)
Maria's sister.
Third daughter of José I. Died (unmarried) in January 1771.

João V (1689–1750)
Maria's grandfather.
Married (1708) Maria Ana von Hapsburg, daughter of Leopold I of Austria. After a major stroke in 1742, he suffered chronic ill-health for the rest of his life. Died in Lisbon in July 1750.

João (later João VI, 1767–1826)
Maria's second son.
Married the Spanish princess, Carlota Joaquina, in 1785. Became crown prince on the death of his elder brother José in 1788. Began to sign documents in his mother's name in 1792. Appointed prince regent in 1799. Inherited the throne in 1816.

João de Bragança (later Duke de Lafões, 1719–1806)
Nephew of João V. Formed an attachment to Maria before her marriage to Pedro.

José I (1714–1777)
Maria's father.
Married Mariana Vitória de Bourbon (daughter of Philip V of Spain) in 1729. Inherited the throne in 1750. Died in Lisbon in February 1777.

José (Crown Prince, 1761–1788)
Maria's elder son.
Firstborn child of Maria I and Pedro III. Married his aunt, Benedita, in February 1777 and became crown prince three days later. Died of smallpox in September 1788.

Maria I (1734–1816)
Eldest daughter of José I and Mariana Vitória de Bourbon.
Married her uncle Pedro in 1760. Inherited the throne in February 1777. Declared insane in 1792. Accompanied her family to Brazil in 1807/8 and died there in 1816. Her body was returned to Lisbon in 1821 and interred in the Basilica da Estrela.

Maria Ana (von Hapsburg, 1683–1754)
Maria's grandmother.
Daughter of Leopold I of Austria. Married João V in 1708. Died in Lisbon in August 1754.

Mariana (1736–1813)
Maria's sister.
Second daughter of José I. Died (unmarried) in Brazil in 1813.

Mariana Vitória (de Bourbon, 1718–1781)
Maria's mother.
Daughter of Philip V of Spain and his second wife, Isabella Farnese. Married José, crown prince of Portugal, in 1729. Acted as regent for the last three months of José's reign. Died in Lisbon in January 1781.

Mariana Vitória (1768–1788)
Maria's daughter.
Married Gabriel de Bourbon (son of Charles III of Spain) in 1785. Gave birth to a son (Pedro Carlos) in June 1786, a daughter in November 1787 (who lived for three days), and a son in October

1788. Died of smallpox on 2 November 1788, followed by her husband and newborn son.

Miguel (1802–1866)
Maria's grandson.
Younger son of Prince João (João VI) and Carlota Joaquina. Instrumental in the outbreak of civil war in 1832. Defeated in 1834 and exiled from the country.

Pedro (Pedro III, 1717–1786)
Maria's husband and uncle.
Younger son of João V, brother of José I. Married Maria in 1760. Acclaimed with her in 1777 and given the title of Pedro III. Died of a stroke in May 1786.

Pedro (later Pedro IV, 1798–1834)
Maria's grandson.
Elder son of Prince João (João VI) and Carlota Joaquina. Married Leopoldina von Hapsburg in 1817. Succeeded his father as Pedro IV in 1826. Won the civil war against his brother Miguel in May 1834. Died four months later in Queluz.

Pedro Carlos (de Bourbon e Bragança, 1786–1812)
Maria's grandson.
Son of Mariana Vitória and Gabriel de Bourbon. Born in Madrid, his parents died of smallpox when he was two years old. Brought to Portugal in 1789. Married his cousin Teresa, eldest daughter of Prince João and Carlota Joaquina, in 1810. Died in Brazil.

Teresa (1793–1874)
Maria's grand-daughter.
First child of Prince João and Carlota Joaquina. Married to her cousin, Pedro Carlos, in 1810. Gave birth to a son (Sebastião) in 1811. Widowed in 1812. Married again in 1838 to her uncle, Charles de Bourbon.

Bourbon Family

Carlota Joaquina (1775–1830)
Maria's daughter-in-law.
Daughter of Charles IV. Married Prince João of Portugal in 1785. Became queen-consort when João inherited the throne in 1816. Died in Lisbon.

Charles III (Carlos III, 1716–1788)
Maria's uncle.
Son of Philip V by his second wife, Isabella Farnese. Succeeded his half-brother, Ferdinand VI. Married Maria Amalia of Saxony.

Charles IV (Carlos IV, 1748–1819)
Maria's first cousin.
Son of Charles III. Married Maria Luísa of Palma. Father of Carlota Joaquina (wife of Prince João of Portugal). Abdicated in 1808 and spent the rest of his life in exile.

Ferdinand VI (Fernando VI, 1713–1759)
Maria's uncle.
Son of Philip V by his first wife, Maria Luisa of Savoy. Married Bárbara, daughter of João V of Portugal, in 1729. The marriage was childless and Ferdinand was succeeded by his half-brother, Charles III.

Gabriel (1752–1788)
Maria's first cousin.
Fourth son of Charles III of Spain. Married Maria's daughter, Mariana Vitória, in 1785. Died of smallpox in 1788. His only surviving child, Pedro Carlos, was brought up in the Portuguese court.

Maria Luísa (1751–1819)
Wife of Charles IV, mother of Carlota Joaquina.

Mariana Vitória (1718–1781)
Maria's mother.
Daughter of Philip V and his second wife, Isabella Farnese. Married José, crown prince of Portugal, in 1729. Died in Lisbon in January 1781.

Pedro Carlos (de Bourbon e Bragança, 1786–1812)
Maria's grandson. See Bragança family.

Philip V (Felipe V, 1683–1746)
Maria's grandfather.
Married first to Maria Luisa of Savoy (1688–1714) and second to Isabella Farnese (1692–1766). Father of Charles III and Mariana Vitória, wife of José I of Portugal.

Aristocrats and Ministers of State

Alorna, Marquis de (1726–1802)
Son-in-law of old Marquis de Távora. Implicated in the Távora conspiracy but spared the scaffold. Released from prison in 1777. Instrumental in the repeal of the guilty sentence on the executed conspirators.

Angeja, 3rd Marquis de (1716–1788)
Brother to Count de São Lourenço. Appointed president of the royal treasury (the most senior secretary of state) in 1777. Partially retired because of ill-health in 1783 but remained in office until his death in March 1788.

Angeja, 6th Marquis de (1788–1827)
Grandson of 3rd Marquis. In Rio de Janeiro at the time of Maria's death in March 1816. Returned to Portugal in 1820.

Atouguia, Count de (1721–1759)
Son-in-law of old Marquis de Távora. Implicated in the Távora conspiracy. Executed in January 1759.

Aveiro, Duke de (1708–1759)
The most powerful nobleman in Portugal. Brother-in-law of old Marquis de Távora. Implicated in the Távora conspiracy. Executed in January 1759.

Carvalho e Melo, Sebastião José de
See Pombal, 1st Marquis de

Marialva, Marquis de (1739–1803)
5th Marquis, known as the young Marquis (son of 4th Marquis, 1713–1799). First lord of the bedchamber, grand master of the horse, and one of Maria's favourite courtiers. Friend of William Beckford.

Melo e Castro, Martinho de (1716–1795)
Ambassador to London (1763–1770). Appointed secretary of state in 1770, retaining this position when Maria came to the throne in 1777.

Mendonça, Diogo de
Appointed secretary of state in 1750. Disgraced in 1756 and exiled to Angola. Died in exile.

Pinto de Sousa Coutinho, Luís (1735–1804)
Ambassador to London (1774–1788). Appointed secretary of state in December 1788. Created 1st Viscount de Balsamão in 1801.

Pombal, 1st Marquis de (1699–1782)
Sebastião José de Carvalho e Melo. Given the titles Count de Oeiras in 1759 and Marquis de Pombal in 1769. Portuguese Ambassador to London (1739–1743) and Vienna (1745–1749). Married Maria Leonor Ernestina, Countess von Daun, in Vienna in 1745. Appointed secretary of state in July 1750. Promoted to first minister in 1756. Fell from power in 1777 and exiled to his estates in central Portugal.

Pombal, 2nd Marquis de (1748–1812)
Elder son of 1st Marquis de Pombal. Allowed to remain at court when his father fell from power in 1777. President of the Lisbon Senate and gentleman of the bedchamber.

Ponte de Lima, Viscount de (1727–1800)
Also known as 14th Viscount de Vila Nova da Cerveira. His father died in prison in 1762. Appointed secretary of state in 1777. Became (acting) president of the royal treasury after the death of 3rd Marquis de Angeja in March 1788. Created Marquis de Ponte de Lima in 1790.

Sá e Melo, Aires de (–1786)
Ambassador to Madrid until appointed secretary of state in 1775. Retained this position when Maria came to the throne in 1777. Became ill in March 1786 and died two months later.

São Lourenço, Count de (1725–1804)
Brother to 3rd Marquis de Angeja. Gentleman of the bedchamber to Pedro. Imprisoned by Pombal in 1760. Released in 1777.

Seabra da Silva, José de (1732–1813)
Secretary of state until his banishment to Angola in 1774. Repatriated in 1777. Appointed secretary of state for home affairs in 1788. Disgraced for a second time by Prince João in 1799. Banished to his country estate.

Távora family:

Old Marquis (3rd Marquis, 1703–1759). Viceroy in India 1750–1755.

Old Marquesa (wife of 3rd Marquis, 1700–1759).

Young Marquis (4th Marquis, 1723–1759). Eldest son of 3rd Marquis.

Young Marquesa (wife of 4th Marquis, 1723–). Mistress of José I. The family was implicated in the attempt to assassinate José I in September 1758, found guilty of treason and executed in January 1759. The young marquesa was spared her life and confined to a convent.

Vila Nova da Cerveira, Viscount de (1683–1762)
13th Viscount (also known as Viscount de Ponte de Lima). Ambassador to Madrid until recalled by Pombal. Arrested in 1760 for opposition to Pombal's administration. Died in prison in 1762. His son became Maria's secretary of state for home affairs in 1777.

Priests

Anunciação, Miguel da (1703–)
Bishop of Coimbra (related to the Távora family). Arrested in December 1768. Released in 1777 to resume his post at Coimbra. Died in office a few years later.

Malagrida, Padre Gabriel (1689–1761)
Jesuit priest. Born in Italy. Worked on a Jesuit mission in Brazil. Present at the deathbed of João V. Banished to Setúbal after writing a treatise on the Lisbon earthquake. Confessor to old Marquesa de Távora. Arrested in December 1758 for involvement in the Távora conspiracy. Executed in September 1761.

Melo, José Maria de (1756–1818)
Appointed Bishop of Algarve in 1787. Appointed confessor to Maria I in December 1788.

Oliveira, Timoteo de
Jesuit priest. Confessor to Maria until banished from court in September 1757. Imprisoned in December 1758 for complicity in the Távora conspiracy. Released in 1777.

São Caetano, Inácio de (1719–1788)
Confessor to Maria I and one of her principal advisers. Given the title Archbishop of Thessalonica. Appointed to Maria's cabinet in August 1787, becoming her chief minister in all but name. Died at Queluz in November 1788.

Vilas Boas, Manuel do Cenáculo (1724–1814)
Appointed Bishop of Beja in 1770. Appointed confessor to Prince José in 1769 and the prince's preceptor in 1770. Dismissed from these offices in 1777 and ordered to reside in his bishopric. Appointed Archbishop of Evora in 1802.

Foreigners

Beckford, William (1759–1844)
Known as the richest commoner in England. Disgraced because of a scandalous affair. Spent time in Portugal in 1787, becoming friends with young Marquis de Marialva. Visited Portugal again in 1793–1795 and 1798–1799.

Bombelles, Marc-Marie, Marquis de (1744–1822)
French ambassador to Portugal, 1786–1788.

Mickle, William Julius (1735–1788)
Scottish poet. Visited Portugal in 1779–1780.

Perez, David (1711–1778)
Italian composer working in the Portuguese court. Teacher of music to Maria and her sisters.

Stephens, Philadelphia (1750/1–1824)
Lived with her brother in Marinha Grande. Wrote an account of the royal visit in 1788.

Stephens, William (1731–1803)
Owner of the royal glassworks in Marinha Grande. Hosted visits by Maria and her family in 1786 and for three days in 1788.

Walpole, the Hon. Robert (1736–1810)
British envoy in Lisbon, 1772–1800. Son of 1st Baron Walpole of Wolterton. Nephew of Sir Robert Walpole (first minister of England) and cousin of Horace Walpole of Strawberry Hill.

Willis, Dr Francis (1717–1807)
Doctor of Medicine with a private lunatic asylum in Lincolnshire. Treated George III of England between October 1788 and March 1789. Treated Maria I of Portugal between March and July 1792.

Notes

Quotations from British envoys and consuls in Lisbon are not referenced in the text. Their letters can be found in the National Archives, Kew (series SP 89 for years up to and including 1780, series FO 63 thereafter). Other quotations are referenced below. Full details of sources can be found in the bibliography.

Introduction

1 Withering, I, 314–315

Part One: Crown Princess

1 Baretti, I, 107
2 Maxwell, 17
3 Whitefield, 12–14
4 Baretti, I, 110
5 Carrère, 75–77
6 Parker (British consul in Oporto), 25 April 1744 (SP 89/43)
7 Wraxall, I, 11
8 Ibid, I, 34
9 Hervey, *Journal*, 125–126, 179
10 Ibid, 179
11 Cormatin, I, 122–123
12 Beckford, *Journal*, 262
13 Whitefield, 5
14 Cheke, *Dictator of Portugal*, 50
15 Thomas Jacomb, 1 November 1755 (Macaulay, *They Went to Portugal*, 273–274)
16 An account by an eye-witness, 11
17 Ibid, 16
18 Ibid, 18
19 *Gentleman's Magazine*, 1756, 67–68
20 Ibid, 1755, 561
21 Wraxall, I, 17
22 Baretti, I, 96–97
23 Cormatin, I, 118
24 Quoted in Kendrick, 137–138
25 Cheke, *Dictator of Portugal*, 110
26 Baretti, I, 180
27 Wraxall, I, 35
28 Laws of Lamego (quoted in Cormatin, II, 215–216)
29 Cormatin, I, 126
30 Baretti, I, 256
31 Cormatin, I, 132
32 Baretti, I, 87, 92–93
33 Ibid, I, 106, 109–111
34 Wraxall, I, 64
35 Maxwell, 102
36 Cormatin, I, 120
37 Beirão, 74–75
38 Beckford, *Journal*, 43
39 Cheke, *Dictator of Portugal*, 238
40 Ibid, 221

Part Two: Absolute Power

1 Cormatin, I, 145, footnote
2 Ibid, I, 29–30
3 Ibid, I, 32
4 Frederick Robinson, Thomas Robinson, July–August 1778 (BA, L30/15/54, L30/17/2)
5 Cormatin, I, 124–125
6 Beirão, 175
7 Ibid, 184
8 Maria I to Charles III, 16 January 1781 (Beirão, 428–429)
9 Quoted in Smith, II, 352–353

10 Beckford, *Journal*, 232–233
11 Maria I to Maria Josefa de Bourbon, 20 January 1783 (Beirão, 439)
12 Ibid, 16 February 1783 (Beirão, 440)
13 Ibid, 6 April 1783 (Beirão, 440)
14 Ibid, 24 April 1783 (Beirão, 442)
15 Maria I to Charles III, 8 May 1785 (Beirão, 436)
16 João to Mariana, 30 May 1785 (Pereira, I, 45)
17 Ibid, 30 May 1785 (Pereira, I, 45–46)
18 Ibid, 17 June 1785 (Pereira, I, 50–55)
19 Wilcken, 52
20 João to Mariana, 4, 19 December 1786 (Pereira, I, 48)
21 Ibid, 14, 24, 28 March 1786 (Pereira, I, 48)
22 Ibid, 28 July 1786 (Pereira, I, 19–21)
23 Beckford, *Italy, with Sketches of Spain and Portugal*, II, 73
24 Bombelles, 185
25 *Lisbon Gazette*, no. 43, 24 October 1786
26 Bombelles, 55, 71
27 Beckford, *Journal*, 104
28 Ibid, 242
29 Ibid, 263–264
30 Ibid, 278
31 Bombelles, 134
32 Philadelphia Stephens, 25 July 1788 (WSRO, Add. MS 8123)
33 Wraxall, I, 37–38
34 Mickle, 15 August 1780 (NLS, 15934–36)
35 Beckford, *Journal*, 222
36 Southey, 19–20. Reprinted by permission of Oxford University Press

Part Three: A Fragile Mind

1 Philadelphia Stephens, 25 July 1788 (WSRO, Add. MS 8123)
2 Bombelles, 134
3 Ibid, 313
4 Charles III to Maria I, 2 November 1788 (Beirão, 366)
5 Ibid, 6 November 1788 (Beirão, 366–367)
6 Beirão, 104
7 Pereira, I, 47
8 Beckford, *Italy, with Sketches of Spain and Portugal*, II, 101
9 Maria I to Queen Maria Luísa, 23 March 1790 (Beirão, 447)
10 Ibid, 6 April 1790 (Beirão, 447)
11 Murphy, 156
12 Pinto, 4 February 1792 (Beirão, 411–412)
13 Ibid, 4 February 1792 (Beirão, 411–412)
14 Ibid, 22 February 1792 (Beirão, 416)
15 Winslow, II, 175
16 Beckford, *Recollections*, 219–220
17 Link, 240
18 Jervis, 28, 29 December 1796 (Tucker, I, 278–280)
19 St Vincent, 24 August 1806 (Tucker, II, 292–293)
20 Brougham, I, 335–336
21 St Vincent, 10 October 1806 (Tucker, II, 302–303)
22 Strangford, 26 September 1807 (Macaulay, *Dom Pedro*, 12)
23 Wilcken, 22–23
24 Ibid, 25
25 O'Neill, 24
26 Ibid, 60–61
27 Santos, I, 218
28 Ibid, I, 218–220
29 Mello Moraes, II, 160
30 Wilcken, 92
31 Luccock, 96–97
32 Ibid, 95
33 Wilcken, 166
34 Mello Moraes, II, 157–158
35 Luccock, 570
36 Wilcken, 246
37 Baillie, II, 76–77

Select Bibliography

Manuscript Sources

Marinha Grande, accounts book, 1786–1802
(CM) Câmara Municipal da Marinha Grande

Mickle, William Julius, miscellaneous papers
(NLS) National Library of Scotland

Portugal, Foreign Office papers (FO 63)
(NA) National Archives

Portugal, State papers (SP 89)
(NA) National Archives

Robinson, Frederick, letters to Anne Robinson, 1778
(BA) Bedfordshire Archives

Robinson, Thomas (Baron Grantham), letters to Frederick Robinson, 1778
(BA) Bedfordshire Archives

Stephens, Philadelphia, account of the royal visit to Marinha Grande, 25 July 1788
(WSRO) West Sussex Record Office

Published Sources

An account by an eye-witness of the Lisbon earthquake of November 1, 1755 (British Historical Society of Portugal, Lisbon, 1985)

Baillie, Marianne, *Lisbon in the Years 1821, 1822 and 1823*, 2 vols (London, 1824)

Baretti, Joseph, *A Journey from London to Genoa, through England, Portugal, Spain and France*, 2 vols (London, 1770)

Barros, Carlos Vitorino da Silva, *Real Fábrica de Vidros da Marinha Grande, II Centenário 1769–1969* (Lisbon, 1969)

Bazin, Hervé, *The Eradication of Smallpox*, trans. Andrew and Glenise Morgan (London, 2000)
Beckford, William, *The Journal of William Beckford in Portugal and Spain 1787–1788*, ed. Boyd Alexander (London, 1954)
—*Recollections of an Excursion to the Monasteries of Alcobaça and Batalha*, ed. Boyd Alexander (Arundel, 1972)
—*Italy, with Sketches of Spain and Portugal*, 2 vols (London, 1834)
Beirão, Caetano Maria de Abreu, *Dona Maria I, 1777–1792*, 2nd edition (Lisbon, 1944)
Bombelles, Marc Marie de, Marquis, *Journal d'un Ambassadeur de France au Portugal, 1786–1788*, ed. Roger Kann (Paris, 1979)
Brougham, Henry, *The Life and Times of Henry, Lord Brougham*, 3 vols (London, 1871)
Carrère, J B F, *A Picture of Lisbon taken on the spot ... by a gentleman many years resident at Lisbon* (London, 1809)
Cheke, Marcus, *Dictator of Portugal: A Life of the Marquis of Pombal* (London, 1938)
—*Carlota Joaquina: Queen of Portugal* (London, 1947)
Cormatin, P M F D, Duke du Châtelet, *Travels of the Duke du Châtelet in Portugal*, ed. J-F Bourgoing, trans. J J Stockdale, 2 vols (London, 1809)
Costigan, Arthur William, *Sketches of Society and Manners in Portugal*, 2 vols (London, 1787)
Croker, Richard, *Travels through Several Provinces of Spain and Portugal* (London, 1799)
Dalrymple, William, *Travels through Spain and Portugal in 1774* (London, 1777)
Duperrier Dumouriez, Charles François, *Etat présent du Royaume de Portugal en l'année 1766* (Lausanne, 1775)
Edmundo, Lúiz, *A Côrte de D. João no Rio de Janeiro (1808–1821)*, 3 vols (Rio de Janeiro, 1939–1940)
Ferro, Maria Inês, *Queluz: The Palace and Gardens* (London, 1997)
Francis, David, *Portugal 1715–1808: Joanine, Pombaline and Rococo Portugal as seen by British Diplomats and Traders* (London, 1985)
Gentleman's Magazine, 1755, 1756
Green, Vivian, *The Madness of Kings: Personal Trauma and the Fate of Nations* (Stroud, 1993)
Hervey, Augustus, *Augustus Hervey's Journal*, ed. David Erskine (London, 2002)

Hervey, Christopher, *Letters from Portugal, Spain, Italy and Germany in the years 1759, 1760 and 1761*, 3 vols (London, 1785)

Inchbold, Stanley, *Lisbon and Cintra* (London, 1907)

Kendrick, T D, *The Lisbon Earthquake* (London, 1956)

Letters from Portugal on the Late and Present State of that Kingdom, anon. but attributed to John Blankett (London, 1777)

Link, Henry Frederick, *Travels in Portugal and through France and Spain* (London, 1801)

Lisbon Gazette (*Gazeta de Lisboa*), various dates

The Lisbon Guide, containing Directions to Invalids who visit Lisbon, anon. (London, 1800)

Luccock, John, *Notes on Rio de Janeiro and the Southern Parts of Brazil taken during a residence of ten years in that country from 1808 to 1818* (London, 1820)

Macaulay, Neill, *Dom Pedro, the Struggle for Liberty in Brazil and Portugal 1798–1834* (Durham, USA, 1986)

Macaulay, Rose, *They went to Portugal* (London, 1946)

—*They went to Portugal Too* (Manchester, 1990)

Maxwell, Kenneth, *Pombal, Paradox of the Enlightenment* (Cambridge, 1995)

Mello Moraes, A J de, *Chronica Geral do Brazil*, 2 vols (Rio de Janeiro, 1886)

Murphy, James, *Travels in Portugal in the years 1789 and 1790* (London, 1795)

O'Neill, Thomas, *A concise and accurate Account of the Proceedings of the Squadron under the Command of Rear-Admiral Sir W S Smith, in effecting the escape and escorting of the Royal Family of Portugal to the Brazils* (London, 1807)

Pereira, Angelo, *D. João VI, Príncipe e Rei*, 4 vols (Lisbon, 1953–58)

Ratton, Jacome, *Recordações: sobre occurrências do sue tempo em Portugal* (London, 1813)

Roberts, Jenifer, *Glass: The Strange History of the Lyne Stephens Fortune* (Chippenham, 2003)

Santos, Luiz Gonçalves dos (Padre Perereca), *Memórias para servir à História do Reino de Brasil*, 2 vols (Rio de Janeiro, 1943)

Saramago, José, *Baltasar and Blimunda*, revised translation by Giovanni Pontiero (London, 2001)

Smith, J A (Count de Carnota), *Memoirs of the Marquis of Pombal*, 2 vols (London, 1934)

Southey, Robert, *Journals of a Residence in Portugal 1800–1801 and a visit to France 1838*, ed. Adolfo Cabral (Oxford, 1960)

Teixeira, José, *O Paço Ducal de Vila Viçosa* (Lisbon, 1983)

Tucker, Jedediah Stephens, *Memoirs of Admiral the Right Hon. the Earl of St Vincent*, 2 vols (London, 1844)

Twiss, Richard, *Travels through Portugal and Spain in 1772 and 1773* (London, 1775)

West, S George, *The Visit to Portugal in 1779–80 of William Julius Mickle* (Lisbon, 1972)

Whitefield, George, *A Brief Account of some Lent and Other Extraordinary Proceedings and Ecclesiastical Entertainments seen last year at Lisbon, in four letters to an English friend* (London, 1755)

Wilcken, Patrick, *Empire Adrift: The Portuguese Court in Rio de Janeiro 1808–1821* (London, 2004)

Winslow, F B, *Physic & Physicians: A Medical Sketch Book*, 2 vols (London, 1839)

Withering, William, *The Miscellaneous Tracts of the Late William Withering MD FRS, written by his son*, 2 vols (London, 1822)

Wraxall, Sir William, *Historical Memoirs of my Own Time*, 2 vols (London, 1815)

Index

Abrantes, 125
Ajuda, hill of, 23, 120
see also Barraca Real
Alcaçarias, baths of, 49, 51, 68, 81, 114, 115
Alcântara, 24, 29
Alcobaça, convent of, 83
Algarve, Bishop of, *see* Melo, José Maria de,
Alorna, Marquis de, 28, 57, 67, 166
American War of Independence, 63
Angeja
  3rd Marquis de, 58, 65, 85, 87, 106, 166
  6th Marquis de, 136, 139, 166
Anglo-Portuguese alliance, 39, 63, 122
Angola, 26, 48
Antouguia, Count de, 28–29, 166
Anunciaçião, Miguel de, 40–1, 54, 64, 168
Aranjuez, 75, 76, 81
Arriaga, Madame, 146
autos-da-fé, 8, 9, 39
Aveiro, Duke de, 28–9, 31, 67, 68, 111, 166

Badajoz, 63, 75
Bahia, 18, 129
Bárbara (daughter of João V), 7, 27, 31, 162
Baretti, Joseph, 6, 24, 36–7
Barraca Real
  building of, 23–4
  destroyed by fire, 120
Bayonne, 125
Beckford, William, 70–1, 81, 84, 85, 86–7, 93–4, 108, 120–1, 169
Belém
  palace of, 8, 13, 14, 16, 21–4
  town of, 20–1, 24, 28–9, 36–7, 79
Bemposta, convent of, 138
Benedita (daughter of José I), 7, 35, 71, 120, 162
  and Prince José, 53, 75, 77, 101, 102–3, 122
  at Marinha Grande, 90, 91, 96, 146, 148, 152, 157
  and Brazil, 126, 132, 133, 137–8
Berlin Decree, 125
Boa Vista (Rio), 132
Bombelles, Marquis de, 83, 87, 103, 169
Botafogo (Rio), 132
Bourbon, Gabriel de, 73–4, 84, 105, 165
Bragança, João de, 32, 163
Bragança dynasty, succession of, 7, 31–2, 53, 109, 112, 119
Brazil, 6, 125–8, 129–38, 141
Buçaco, 35

Cabo, Nossa Senhora do, 73
Caldas da Rainha, 9–10, 68, 79, 82–3, 84, 97, 146, 153, 156
  provedor's house in, 82, 87
Campo Pequeno (bullring), 36
Carlos III, *see* Charles III
Carlos IV, *see* Charles IV
Carlota Joaquina, 120, 124, 141, 162, 164
  marriage of, 73–5, 91, 103–4, 109, 110–1, 112, 119, 122
  appearance and behaviour of, 75, 77, 78–9, 83, 87, 90, 122

at Marinha Grande, 90, 146, 148, 152, 155, 157
and Brazil, 126, 132, 133, 137–8
Carvalho e Melo, Sebastião de, *see* Pombal, 1st Marquis de
Caya, river, 34, 62, 63, 75
Charles III (of Spain), 73, 75, 104–5, 165
Charles IV (of Spain), 109, 111, 165
Cintra, *see* Sintra
Clementina (daughter of Maria I), 48, 51
Coimbra
Bishop of, *see* Anunciaçião, Miguel de,
town of, 45, 93, 109, 119, 158
university of, 44–5, 151
College of Nobles, 44
Constitution, the, 137–8
Corpus Christi, procession of, 61, 118
Cumberland, Duke of, 32

Dom João VI (flagship), 138
Dom José de Alvarado, comedy of, 151
Doroteia (daughter of José I), 7, 43–4

Elvas, 63, 75
Estoril, 50
Estrela, 64
abbess of, 81, 105, 106, 108, 113, 116
church (basilica) of, 64, 138–40
convent of, 68–9, 81
Evora, 74

Falmouth, 24
Felipe V, *see* Philip V
Ferdinand VI (of Spain), 7, 27, 107–8, 165
French Revolution, 109–10, 111, 122, 137

Gabriel de Bourbon, *see* Bourbon, Gabriel de
George III (of England), 101, 107, 109, 116
Goa, 18
Graça, convent of, 15–6, 23

Holy Inquisition, the, 8, 39, 40
Holy Week, processions of, 7–8

Jervis, Admiral Sir John (Lord St Vincent), 123, 124–5
Jesuits, 6, 15, 46, 64
and Pombal, 25–7, 28, 30, 35, 40, 42, 44–5
and Maria I, 23, 64
João V, 5–11, 16, 32, 70, 74, 162
bastard sons of, 7, 35, 54
João, Prince (João VI), 40, 60, 87, 120, 123, 140, 141, 162
marriage of, 73–6, 77–9, 103–4, 109, 110–1, 112, 119
and death of father, 79–81
at Marinha Grande, 90, 91, 95, 148, 150, 153, 155
illnesses of, 71–2, 101, 102, 109, 124
and madness of mother, 1–2, 113, 116, 117, 118–9
and Napoleonic Wars, 122–5
and Brazil, 125–8, 129–32, 134, 136–8
Johnson, Dr Samuel, 6
José I, 5, 7, 10–1, 12–4, 32–3, 36–7, 82, 163
and Lisbon earthquake, 21–3
and Távora conspiracy, 18, 27–30
and Marquis de Pombal, 16–7, 25–7, 31, 41, 46–8, 51, 53
assassination attempts on, 27–30, 38, 41–3
inauguration of statue of, 49–50
illness and death of, 48–51, 52–3, 54
José, (Crown) Prince, 38, 60, 71, 84, 86, 87, 106, 163

education of, 43, 46–7, 103
and Benedita, 53, 75, 77, 91, 96, 103
at Marinha Grande, 90, 148, 152
death of, 79, 101, 102–3

Lamego, Laws of, 31–2, 59
Leiria, 91, 96, 147, 149, 150–1, 153, 156
Letrado Avarento, farce of, 151
Lincolnshire, 116
Lisbon, 6
earthquake in, 19–24
rebuilding of, 39–40, 65
royal palace in, 5, 7, 8, 14, 23, 40
Lisbon Gazette, 83, 109–10
Lobo, José, 146
London, 16, 106, 114
Louis XV (of France), 104
Louis XVI (of France), 112
Luanda, 48

Macau, 18
Madrid, 27, 35, 75, 86, 87, 104
Mafra, convent-palace of, 8, 13, 72, 112, 122
Malagrida, Gabriel, 10, 17, 25–6, 28, 38–9, 168
Maria I, 5–10, 12–3, 15–6, 36–7, 42, 71–2, 163
and Lisbon earthquake, 21–4
and Távora conspiracy, 28–9, 31
marriage of, 31–5
children of, 38, 40–1, 43–4, 48, 51, 52
and the succession, 46–8, 52, 53–4, 57–61
policies of, 62–3, 64–6
and Marquis de Pombal, 31, 66–7, 68, 69
and marriages of children, 53, 63, 64, 73–6, 77–8, 110–1
and Estrela, 64, 68–9, 110
and protocol, 70–1, 103
bereavements of, 79–83, 86–8, 102–3, 104–5
at Marinha Grande, 83, 89–98, 145–58
and French Revolution, 109–10, 111, 122
madness of, 1–2, 108, 112, 113–9, 120, 121, 122
and Brazil, 126–8, 129–35, 136–7
funeral of, 138–40
Maria Ana (wife of João V), 5, 7, 10, 11, 16–8, 163
Maria Luísa (wife of Charles IV), 110–1, 165
Marialva, Marquis de, 70–1, 86, 87, 94, 110, 117, 148, 167
Mariana (wife of José I), 8, 12, 13–4, 36–7, 42, 163, 165
marriage and children of, 5, 7, 104
and Maria's marriage, 31–2, 34, 35
and Pombal, 46–8, 57–8
regency of, 51–2, 54
visit to Spain of, 62–3
illness and death of, 48–9, 63, 68
Mariana (daughter of José I), 7, 35, 120, 163
at Marinha Grande, 90, 146, 148, 152–3, 155, 157
and Brazil, 126, 132, 134, 136, 138
Mariana (daughter of Maria I), 41, 79, 104, 163–4
marriage of, 73–6, 77–8
children of, 81, 84, 86–7, 104–5
Marinha Grande, 82–3, 84, 88, 89–97, 109, 145–58
Melo, José Maria de, 108, 113–4, 117, 118, 168
Melo e Castro, Martinho de, 58, 85, 86, 87, 106, 167
Mendonça, Diogo de, 26, 166
Mickle, William Julius, 57, 93, 169
Miguel (grandson of Maria I), 126–7, 133, 137–8, 141, 164
Monte Real, 95, 150
Morocco, 12

Napoleonic Wars, 122–5, 137
Nazaré, village of, 96, 101, 152, 153
Nossa Senhora da Ajuda, convent of (Rio), 134, 136
Nossa Senhora de Candelária (Rio), 137

Octavius, Prince (son of George III), 101
Odivelas, convent of, 7
Oeiras
  Count de, *see* Pombal, 1st Marquis de
  Pombal's house in, 50, 53, 58, 59, 72
Oliveira, Timotei de, 26, 28, 57, 168
Olympia (Voltaire), 82
Oporto, 48

Papal nuncio, 15, 26, 34, 41, 43, 44, 64, 68
Patriarch, the, 6, 22, 36–7
Patriarchal church (Lisbon), 10, 23
Pedras Negras (Luanda), 48
Pedro, Prince (Pedro III), 7, 11, 37, 59–60, 65, 74–5, 164
  marriage of, 32–4, 35, 46
  illness and death of, 62, 68, 72–3, 79–81
Pedro (Pedro IV, grandson of Maria I), 126–7, 132, 133, 137, 141, 164
Pedro Carlos (grandson of Maria I), 81, 109, 110, 126, 132, 133–4, 164, 165
Pele, João Baptiste, 50–1, 66
Peninsular War, 137
Perez, David, 15, 35, 63, 169
Pernambuco, 137
Philip V (of Spain), 107–8, 165
Pinto de Sousa Coutinho, Luís, 106, 107, 109, 111, 114–5, 167
Pombal, 1st Marquesa de, 16, 59
Pombal, 1st Marquis de, 32, 36–7, 41, 49–50, 70, 167
  rise to power of, 16–7, 25–7
  and Lisbon earthquake, 22
  and Távora conspiracy, 27–30
  and Maria's marriage, 34–5
  and the church, 31, 40–1, 44
  and Jesuits, 28, 30, 38–9, 40, 44–5
  and Seven Years War, 39
  and rebuilding of Lisbon, 39–40, 49
  and South America, 62
  and the succession, 46–8, 53
  and acts of tyranny, 28–9, 42–3, 50–51, 52
  fall of, 51–2, 54, 57–8, 59, 61
  trial of, 66–7
  death of, 69, 70
Pombal, 2nd Marquis de, 69, 72, 156, 167
Pombaline, architectural style, 40
Ponte de Lima, Viscount de, 58, 65, 71, 85, 86, 87, 89, 106, 117, 145
Pope, the, 6, 44–5, 64, 116
Príncipe Real (flagship), 126–30

Queluz, palace of, 32–3, 61–2, 63, 68, 72, 77–8, 102, 104–5, 109, 111–2, 119–20, 138
  entertainments at, 33, 35–6, 39, 44
  and Maria's illness, 117, 122, 126

Real Mesa Censória, 40
Ricketts, Captain, 124
Rio de Janeiro, 6, 18, 48, 129–38
Rocha, Padre, 149
Royal Academy of Sciences, 66

Sá e Melo, Aires de, 58, 85, 167
Salic law, 13, 46
Salitri Theatre (Lisbon), 87, 93
Salvador de Bahia, *see* Bahia
Salvaterra de Magos, 1–2, 8, 13–4, 24, 29, 44, 46–8, 49, 51, 67, 71–2, 87, 109, 112–4

Santa Engracia, Devotion of, 29, 47
São Caetano, Inácio de, 66, 69, 86, 105, 106, 108, 139, 168
  at Marinha Grande, 89–90, 145, 147, 149, 157
São Lourenço, Count de, 34–5, 57, 58, 81, 167
São Vicente de Fora, church of, 10, 57, 79, 102, 138
Seabra e Silva, José de, 46–8, 54, 106, 167
Sebastião (great-grandson of Maria I), 134
Senate House (Lisbon), 2, 68, 74, 85, 114
Senhor dos Passos, statue of, 15–6, 23, 47
Sésostris, tragedy of, 93–4, 148, 154
Setúbal, 26, 73
Seven Years War, 38–9
Silva, Nicolau Luís da, 82
Sintra, 122
  palace of, 8, 61, 86
smallpox, 71–2, 79, 101–2, 152
Society of Jesus, *see* Jesuits
Sousa, João de, muleteer, 42
South America, 26
  territorial disputes with Spain, 62
St Vincent, Lord, *see* Jervis, Admiral Sir John
Stephens, Jedediah, 145
Stephens, Lewis, 145
Stephens, Philadelphia, 89–97, 145–58, 169
Stephens, William, 24, 82–3, 87–8, 89–97, 145–58, 169

Tagus, river, 2, 9, 20–1, 29, 43, 74, 127
Tartuffe (Molière), 40
Távora
  conspiracy of, 27–30, 66, 108, 113
  family of, 28–9, 40, 67, 68, 167–8
  old Marquesa de, 18, 28–9
  old Marquis de (3rd Marquis), 14, 18, 28–9, 57
  young Marquesa de, 14, 18, 27
  young Marquis de (4th Marquis), 18, 28–9
Teresa (grand-daughter of Maria I), 134, 164
Trafaria, village of, 52
treasure fleet, 18

Vatican, the, 6, 34, 41
Vendas Novas, palace of, 74
Versailles, 32
Vienna, 16
Vieira, Foz de, 150
Vila Nova de Cerveira, Viscount de, 34–5, 58, 168
Vila Nova da Rainha, town of, 9, 85
Vila Viçosa, palace of, 8, 13, 38, 41–2, 62, 63, 74–6, 94, 141
Vilas Boas, Manuel do Cenáculo, 43, 46, 64, 103, 169
Voltaire, 7, 82

Walpole, the Hon. Robert, 45, 47–8, 52, 65, 71, 107, 169
War of the Two Brothers, 141
Willis, Dr Francis, 107, 113, 115, 116–9, 129, 169